STARTING A NEW LIFE FULL OF ENCOURAGEMENT

THE POWER OF A FRESH PERSPECTIVE

DAYSSY DAVILA

ISBN-10: 1-945719-01-X
ISBN-13: 978-1-945719-01-1

Edited by: **Marc Shamus**
Published by: **i Master Life Publishing**

Check out more of our books at:

iMasterLife.com

TABLE OF CONTENTS

SECTION I

GOD & GRACE

TABLE OF CONTENTS

SECTION II
VALUES

SECTION III
MINDSET

TABLE OF CONTENTS

TABLE OF CONTENTS

SECTION IV
ACTION STEPS

TABLE OF CONTENTS

PERSONAL MESSAGE FROM MARC SHAMUS

I love the humanitarian spirit that is at the core of Dayssy Davila. She is a shiny gem that creates a ray of hope onto so many women who have felt the void of living a happy life. Like a breath of fresh air, she brings in much needed and refreshing winds of change through her inspiring words.

For many years, my wife and I have been blessed to have Dayssy be a part of our life. She chooses to have a positive uplifting outlook on life possibilities. Her vision of helping people improve the quality of their own life experience is an example of the beacon she is and how valuable of an asset she becomes for those around her.

If you are a woman who has endured far too much pain and seeks to gain a fresh perspective, this book from Dayssy is 100% for you. She is a woman who has walked in your shoes, overcame her own adversities and ascended to a new life filled with abundance and incredible encouragement.

I hope you read this book in its entirety and apply ideas Dayssy shares from her heart with you. Trust me, even if a few of her concepts work for you, this is enough to make a worthwhile paradigm shift in your life for the better. On my behalf, thank you Dayssy for all the heart felt things you do for others to love them and help them heal.

WHY I WROTE THIS BOOK

I wrote this book because I'm the daughter of God and three year ago I started my new, exciting life. I have been filled with so much encouragement along with a refreshing, new found sense of purpose. Perhaps, you are like me, and need a positive shift in your life to get you to that happy place.

There are many reasons you might want to start a new life, and many ways you could approach this decision. For example, perhaps you just ended a relationship and have to figure out how to get started with a new, healthy, happy life away from your partner, or perhaps you just don't like where you live and want to move to find a new start in a new community.

Regardless of your goals or reasons for change, it's possible to start fresh if you think carefully, plan thoroughly, and check in with yourself to make sure you're doing okay. Life can be an absolutely blissful experience, if we let it be. It truly is just a reframing of perspective coupled with proactive choices.

As for me, I love to help people. The start of my new life began with my decision to open a non-profit organization. Through this, every day I began working on helping many people live their dreams. I was there to assist them in feeling better as they moved past their difficult times.

I love transforming the life of my clients so that they feel empowered to take on the world and pursue their dreams. In the writing of **STARTING A NEW LIFE FULL OF**

WHY I WROTE THIS BOOK

ENCOURAGEMENT, I am able to teach concepts that helped me turn my life around and start a very blessed, new life.

WHY YOU SHOULD READ THIS BOOK

As you read this book, be open to experiencing a life transformation. Be honest to yourself where you are currently at in your life at this moment in time. Be motivated to absorb ideas I lay out for you. They can be the stimulator for big, visible and much needed modifications in your life.

This book will help you gain the knowledge of the various methods which can work to your advantage. It will give you some of the top resolutions to cause wondrous results. It will then be up to you to utilize practicing these lessons taught in this book, **STARTING A NEW LIFE FULL OF ENCOURAGEMENT**. You must put in the effort and take action to get a desirable outcome.

You can take your life from dreary gloom to blossoming bloom with this newly discovered insights. What you opt to do with this is completely your choice. I am cheering you on all the way as you read this book and start on the journey to your new life full of encouragement… Welcome to the <u>NEW</u> YOU!!

PERSONAL DEDICATION

To my dear GOD. This is the humblest sentence. Without God I'm nothing and with GOD I'm everything.

To my Dear Grandma Dra. Blanca Bravo, to my dear Father Dr. Rodrigo Davila and my dear Mother Ms. Dayssy Zuniga de Davila, and my two children, Rodrigo Luzuriaga and Emmamuel Luzuriaga.

They are all precious gifts from GOD. They are my life; my everything. I admire their resistance and determination to press past every obstacle and move forward in life through the faith they have. This faith encourages them through life as they know everything will turn out for the best

They have a legacy in the highest GOD, and your latter will be greater than your former. I declare that each of you shall walk in the fullness of your purpose and destiny. I'm thankful that nights turned into mornings; and friends turned into family and dreams turned into reality.

Amen.

Dayssy with sons Rodrigo Luzuriaga and Emmamuel Luzuriaga

INTRODUCTION

I'm a woman that never gives up. All the experiences I've had with different women who were victims of domestic violence proved to be extremely valuable. The time that I spent with the ladies was always unique and taught me just as many valuable lessons as I feel it did for them.

For me, this is a gift, because I realize they need love, encouragement and lots of good hope. I encourage their heart to start a new life. Suddenly, out of the blue, I decided to write my first book. This is sweetest way to say from the bottom of my heart that I'm here for you.

That's what Encouragement is all about. Each page in this book, **STARTING A NEW LIFE FULL OF ENCOURAGEMENT**, has an amazing message of hope to brighten your day and let you know how much I care. As you read, I hope you'll remember forever all of the amazing gifts and talents that you have.

Also, you'll realize you are a valuable person. You deserve the best in this world because GOD created you and sent you into this world for a great purpose. Please, always remember, you are very special person and he is by your side, just as I am, too!

I will cover in this book lessons that I have learned that assisted me in Starting a New Life Full of Encouragement. Each lesson is important for you to master and be able to leverage your own life to create big victories. Remember, it is important that you gain a fresh perspective to kick start these changes in your life.

Without further ado, here we go…

Dayssy Davila

SECTION I
<u>GOD & GRACE</u>

1. GOD IS ENCOURAGEMENT, SO LEAN ON HIM AND BECOME INSPIRED

GOD controls the universe. I'm born in Ecuador and grew up there, but my family decided to move to the USA. Some circumstances pushed me towards my new destiny. Since the beginning, I wanted to start a business and with creativity I launched my first business 15 years ago. I began it with a strong vision, prayer and massive action. I also applied to receive the license for the construction company to start working in the USA.

My goal at the beginning was to create my primary income with many construction projects. Little by little, we worked on larger projects. The work involved more opportunity to expand. We even had the opportunity to do work at the Pentagon after the 09/11 catastrophe. Immediately, we had positive reactions from clients and the community. It propelled us to grow more and more. Now I develop projects all around the world. Very incredible, but it's true. God is in control of our destiny.

I realize that everyone comes to this world with a purpose. Creating a new you will make a statement that you are ready to fulfill your purpose. GOD makes sure that everything will be given to you, even a new way to see the world and become a better person in the process. Be unique and strong. Be confident and the rest of the fine details will come to you. You have big potential to do something new that you never have done before.

It's the power of the universe inside of you. See this fascinating world as full of large opportunities. This mean you have the power to define how you think as well as how you are going to see the new world. This is very simple. It will help you to get access to resources you were unaware of beforehand. Create this new life because GOD wants you to live a good life.

Choose to focus on God's goodness rather than on your circumstances. GOD will encourage you when you need things to be better. He will assist in that change and help you to obtain economic freedom. Today, live above your situation because the upward look with your head held high, it looks the best on YOU.

Please review Jeremiah 33:3. In this passage, we see that blessings affect how others connect with you. Large doors swing on little hinges. How important is your act of faith? Monumental! In fact, your act of faith releases the hand of God to you. The number 3:33 represent certain promises of GOD. These are promises that he has already made but has not yet come to pass. I sternly believe these will be released by your faith now.

If all of us learned to focus with extreme responsibility to obey God's commandments, miracles would happen more often. What is most important is the process to transform us. Let GOD inspire you. Pray not just on Sunday or at bed time. Use power of prayer always. That Means Now! Power of Prayer works. As you start to transition, this leads to transformation. Do you remember your transition from the kindergarten to the high school or perhaps and from being single to being married?

In life, you may have different assignments you need to work on. When you <u>believe</u> God is in your corner, nothing is difficult. This <u>belief</u> gives you 1,000 fold the strength to go on and make it happen. You must embrace the transition process so you can experience the desired transformation. Enlarge your belief and have a personal evolution.

You can't sustain miraculous victories without him, the power of your faith will raise you and your family. Watch carefully, as God will demonstrate his power to you over and over throughout your life. Sometimes I ask him, "I need your help in order to get a successful transformation in my life" and he answers my prayers.

For example: I remember one of my best days in my life was when GOD led me to follow him. I was in JERUSALEM and so many people mentioned to me that I will feel something different. Honestly, I didn't experience anything until the very last day there. My group decided to visit the old town and for some reason we became lost.

We stumbled across a church that grabbed my attention, although I'm not sure what compelled me to stop there. No-one can explain what happened next! When I got inside the church, something incredibly beautiful happened.

Once I entered the building, I began to feel something supernatural inside of me. My inner child was set free and felt at peace. On the floor right below me was the tomb of JESUS. Wow!!

At that moment, I forgot about everything around me. All that I was aware of was the energy I was experiencing.

I put my knees on the floor and had an immediate divine connection between GOD and I. There was this extreme pleasure I felt inside of my heart. It was the most important day as God opened my eyes, because I was completely blind before then. Since that day, I have a very strong bond with GOD.

Emotionally, before this day, I was in limbo for so many aspects of my life. I was thinking money is more important than anything. Now, I think different. Money is important ONLY when you have the opportunity to help others. Since that day, my life changed completely. I received the unconditional love from GOD, in all aspects. I ask him every day, "please GOD, give me the capacity to impact this world; give me the ability to encourage others."

I can speak words loaded with wisdom, passed to me via GOD. Leave your mark on this generation. GOD will enlarge your mind and provide you the capacity to discern all you will ever need. I have a big purpose in this world and will align with it with the power of GOD. Of course, I choose to follow him and since that miraculous day, many blessing have come into my life every single day.

I ensure that my life has positive encouragement. I use different strategies to enlarge my heart. The first thing I do is recognize that GOD gives us so many talents. We all have the capacity to grow in different levels; spirit, soul and body. Yes, GOD wants us to be spiritually sound and make him the Lord of our lives. He wants us to live without limitations

2. HOLD ON TO GOD'S LOVE

Some people think happiness comes only from consistency of working in the same job at the same place long term. While I was traveling for an entire year and living abroad, it became a very compelling experiment that led to much creativity and learning experiences. I learned that happiness can also come from having variety and developing many new skills to go along with this.

Who knows what work you will pursue in the future, but perhaps you could be best suited being your own next boss, and for your own company, just like I did. Listen to my practical and encouraging message. Believe in the one who knows you the best and loves you most; you. Dare to live your life to the fullest, because the world needs you, your hopes and your dreams.

I have followed the advice of personal mentors and have learned so much. I've watched motivational videos every day for about 3 years now and I love the inspiration and blessings that it has on me with those words. For this, thank you GOD. My worth and value is in my relationship with Jesus. My joy and peace only comes from Him alone. Amen. Keep moving forward in life is so important. Choose instinctively and stay conscious of yourself and your surroundings.

Have vision and see your future. No overthinking things. Let your conscious mind wander and brainstorm all incoming thoughts.

STARTING A NEW LIFE FULL OF ENCOURAGEMENT

Faith will create a great impact on your life. For example, always paint a picture in your mind and use your pre-invested time to visualize your future like an artist - or a famous actor. One of the greatest needs we all have is feeling encouragement to continue on the path that we are on. The faith will drive us further to achieve more.

Make the visual images as crystal clear be possible. Embrace your flaws, nobody's perfect but God wants us to have a pure heart. You can watch me and think, "If she can do it, I can do it!" Yes, of course you can. Know that you are valued, important, and that your life matters.

Back in my childhood, I learned to start my life with faith. I'm using role models such as my Mother and Grandmother. I use the same type of power values like they did. I'm old school. Sometimes, I make notes as I learn from others, so I'm always ready when I have a meeting. I Love to prepare everything and be in control of as many elements as possible of my outcome.

Sometimes, however, you can't control things, but your preparation and belief in GOD makes the difference. GOD is in control of our lives to help us to keep moving forward. Put value on achievements and enjoy your possessions. Feel important when you have accomplishments, such as a new fancy car. Conversely, your self-worth should not be tied only to material things or to temporary situations that may change quickly as time goes on.

Some people don't have values and will either gloat on accomplishments with no glory to GOD or want to belittle you for your accomplishments. If you find people behaving in that way, don't feel disappointment if someone hurts your feelings. Get your self-worth from the right place. Be proud of what you are because you are so valuable. GOD said, "you are important and there is nothing you can do to change people." Just close that door and know that GOD will open thousands of other doors for you.

Be confident on what you have because you are worth it. God has made you an extraordinary human-being. The act of giving is the soul of living. I am a woman of many talents, and the guardian of my children. I have the strength of my God, to lead me through whatever Life has in store for me.

I shall look ahead, rather than be pulled back to past sorrows or mistakes, for only by moving forward can I begin anew. I will pray for those I love, that my love may be their blessings, that my prayers will be their strength. It's time to do something different in your life.

Love also can change your life. I have learned this lesson the hard way. I have always thought everyone was capable of loving another human being. I have realized that my friends, family and I are capable. When someone cannot love you or stay with you, it's not because of you, it's because they just can't. Love them and let them go. Do not try and make them love you. It's not in their nature. Do not blame yourself.

Surround yourself with people who show you love. These are the ones that are there for you when you are at your worst. These people stay through the tough stuff. They are the people that call when they say they will, and text, just to let you know they care.

It is the people that actually show up and don't make excuses. These are the people that love you, and allow you to love them. Cherish them! Let them know how they have affected your life.

Thank you Jesus for your love. Remember LORD has chosen you to be his treasured possession. (Deuteronomy 14:2, NIV) The act of giving is the soul of living.

3. BE GRATEFUL

Every day you need to say, "This is a new day. This a new beginning in my life." Open you heart and he will give you wisdom, strength, favor, and joy. Be grateful! Life is too short. Every situation can change. Always be passionate and live with respect and Integrity. God tests our morals. Think, it's not the adversity. It's how we handle the adversity through positive reinforcements in our life.

Everything is a process. Pray for new doors to open for you that you never thought possible. God will do beyond what you ever imagined in every area of your life! All the time, I say to my people, "I'm here when you need me with a helping hand, with a listening ear, a shoulder to lean on. I want to remind you that if life throws you a curve ball, you can still hit a home run and I'm cheering you on."

Stick your neck out and focus on consistent discipline to archive your goals and your dreams. Trust on God, and through faith in God, he provides the direction to correction. God will offer the protection in life. Live with a winning attitude. Have a lot of perseverance. It also doesn't hurt to receive a little help from your friends. You can make it through anything.

STARTING A NEW LIFE FULL OF ENCOURAGEMENT

You can climb the highest mountain, solve the hardest puzzle, conquer your fears, and even reach the stars as long as you never stop learning. If you want to succeed, you need to develop four basic, but important competencies:

1) Creating positive personal impact

2) Become a consistent high performer

3) Communication skills

4) Relationship building

Lifelong learning is the first step in becoming super competent. In today's fast paced world, if you don't keep learning, you're actually not standing still, you're really falling behind.

One of my favorite quotes from Mahatma Gandhi nails it when it comes to lifelong learning. He said, "Live as if you were to die tomorrow. Learn as if you were to live forever." The common sense point here is simple. Successful people are outstanding performers.

Outstanding performers remain outstanding performers by becoming lifelong learners. They continually expand their knowledge in order to get out in front of the pack and stay there. Begin your lifelong learning journey by focusing on your strengths and working to improve them every day.

Building on your strengths is easier than overcoming your weaknesses. When you build on your strengths you can make incremental improvements. However, if you have a glaring gap in your skills, address it now. Don't wait to take necessary quantum leaps. How do you plan on learning it? Remember what Ben Franklin had to say, "An investment in knowledge pays the best interest."

4. STAY PURE AND BE OBEDIENT TO GOD

Purity and obedience go hand in hand. I trust God whole heartedly on this. For a lot of years, I have served Him, in spite of being held up by circumstantial issues of life. I thank God for the assurance to keep believing, no matter what comes my way. For doing so creates a true wonderland of joy for us.

I am where I am because I'm never tired of dreaming and staying true to myself and God. A life of purity involves more than the things we do and don't do. It includes our thoughts and words too. The angels are saying that you really need rest to revive your energy; as it takes a large amount of energy to become a new you. This is a new beginning.

A life of purity means living in obedience to God's Word with our thoughts, our words, and our deeds. And that will benefit you, your loved ones, and your career. Watching a meditation video to motivate yourself is important. Today I pray that God will give you wisdom, strength, favor, and joy. I pray doors will open for you that you never thought possible and that God will do beyond what you ever imagined in every area of your life.

One of my biggest motivations is my unique and incredible Mother who is an utmost, excellent professional. She always shares her amazing heart that is full of joy. When I feel the love from her, it makes me hopeful to do better for this world. My heart is full of joy, because the Professional Associations of Women in my birth country Ecuador recognized my Mother as a Mother Symbol. I Could not agree more and that's why she is my strongest motivation.

Mom dedicated her life to raising good citizenship through education, to develop awareness of the issues we face, to help grow people's moral values and teach that our responsibility is to pass different values of empathy and kindness to our family. We need to show our children that humanity is the essence of compassion and is the beginning of morality.

Imagining what it is like to be someone other than yourself. This is at the core of our humanity. It is the essence of compassion, and it is the beginning of morality. I'm getting better and better every day in every way. Regret nothing! Life is too short to worry about crazy things. Have fun! Love yourself and love others. Love is happiness and it does not depend on your circumstances. It's a choice that you make.

Also make sure to thank the people who make your life happy in so many ways. Sometimes, I forget to tell people how much I really appreciate them for being an important part of my life. So if you are reading this, know I love you. Make sure you don't forget to let people in your life know just how much you care.

You deserve to be happy; not in the arms of someone who keeps you waiting, but in the arms of the one who will take your love forever. Don't wait, as your time is far too valuable. I Offer to God some sacrifices and honor him. I pray with my all my heart.

As for God, I say prayers like," Please, my dear God, protect me and my family. Cover me with love and blessings. Also, provide me and protect me with peace, happiness, health, and wealth and other life richness, because it's only in your hands, my dear GOD. I love you because you created me with one purpose and sent me to this world for one mission and many thanks for all your blessings."

Always remember God's great love for us. May this day bring new meaning and changes in your life. We go for these external material things thinking they're going to bring us happiness, but it's backwards. You need to go for the inner joy, the inner peace, and the inner vision first, and then all of the outer things start to appear. I hope your day has been going well for you, my dear friends. If not, I hope it gets better. You are an amazing person who will inspire others to do great things, so keep up the hard work.

I know you may feel unimportant or insecure at the moment but know that you are a beautiful human being inside and out and that you are important. Just remember to work on the internal message. We just need to craft a positive message to ourselves. You are so valuable and important! I hope this idea will help you a bit, just as much as it has done over time for me.

5. PRACTICE FORGIVENESS

You need to practice letting go. Forgiving someone can be a really difficult task. It's also a very important decision. Realize people are human and they are going to make mistakes. Sometimes people have a hard time letting go. When it comes to you, don't be too hard on yourself. Let go of as much negativity as possible.

Forgive people that may wrong you and move on, because each day is a new beginning. Each day is a new opportunity to start a new life. If you don't let go of your resentment, the lingering emotional effects are anger, bitterness, and turmoil.

Forgiveness also makes you more compassionate towards others. We can't do anything about the past, but we can change our future with the way we think. You have a full possible potential and you can start a new life with a magnificent future. Today starts a new future with many new opportunities.

I totally understand why many people end up going through life with low self-esteem while pretending everything is ok. Living day by day with your head down is no way to exist. You need to encourage yourself to change and go to the next level. Follow your destiny by following your dreams. Listen to your inner voice because you have something great inside of you. You have big potential and your life assignment is waiting to take shape. Of course, this isn't easy, but nothing is impossible in this world.

6. COUNT YOUR BLESSINGS

Every day, count your blessings and spread love to someone you love. Give free compliments to all you come into contact with, including those you barely know. Tell your partner that they look great today.

Compliment your coworker's new hairdo, or tell the cashier at the grocery store that you like her earrings. Possibly, you can go even deeper, and compliment important aspects of people's personalities.

Since we live in a consumer culture that preaches discontentment, people have been subconsciously taught to socially attack gratitude. Let's break this insane attack pattern and bring rise to an attitude of gratitude.

Give at least one compliment a day and you will see that other people have so much to offer to the world. As you gain inner peace, you feel more positive, which helps you become a better person.

Find a private, safe space free from distractions. Sit in a comfortable position. Clear your mind of any formal thoughts, and take a few deep, slow breaths. Observe the thoughts in your head. Don't feel or react, just observe. If your focus breaks, just count to ten. Meditate until you feel cleansed and rejuvenated.

Decide to be grateful. If something doesn't turn your way, try to change what you can, smile, stay positive, and move on. No matter how much you achieve in life, you will always feel unhappy if you constantly focus on what you don't have. Instead, devote time every day to appreciating the things you do have.

Think beyond material items; appreciate your loved ones, and remember happy memories. Pray and/or meditate. Praying to a higher power or meditating can help cultivate the qualities you seek to embody.

Meditation and prayer can help you find inner peace and focus on your inner self. As you increase your self-awareness, you understand what you really want and find clarity in your life.

7. BE EMPATHETIC

Being empathetic includes all the feelings that you have like thoughts, or attitudes towards others. Realize that being kind, understanding, and compassionate in how you treat other people is largely the result of having a loving and caring attitude about others.

Try to put yourself in other people's shoes and see things from their perspective. Ask yourself, "How would I feel if I were the other person. You will likely act with the other person's feelings in mind. This will show in your words and actions. Be kind to other people, not so you look good to others, but more so that other people may benefit from your selfless acts.

It doesn't work very well if you are merely trying to be diplomatic. Don't adopt a policy like, "Anything for a quiet life." Honestly, all of us have wisdom that creates answers. Ask for wisdom from GOD to deal with the challenges transpiring today and tomorrow. You will receive the confidence needed to assist you.

It's your life; no one else's. Don't wish your life was easier; wish you were better. Be strong women! It is good to remember your past pain to push you to the victory if you are close to a goal. However, I've honestly blocked out a lot of negative memories. Personally I have found these don't serve me if I think about them <u>all the time</u>.

I also don't let the noise of other's people opinions of me drag me down. Always follow your own inner voice. Have the courage to follow your heart and intuition. Those other people most likely do not pay your bills, manage the tasks in your daily life for you, nor do they know enough about the struggles you have graciously faced in your life to get to the point you are today.

In life, sometimes we experience difficult times. Regardless, you need to know that these challenges will not stay forever. Know that your destiny will be the best and then start fully believing in yourself again. It is helpful to remember those moments that brought tears of happiness to your eyes, when your heart opened up and you felt a great surge of love with a connection far beyond the physical.

I use and follow encouraging words based on what God says. You should do the same. Tell yourself:

1) I believe that one day, God will bring passion into my life because he is my father.

2) He is the creator of the universe and he is in control of my life. He always brings me in the right direction.

3) I'm so thankful for the many blessings that the Lord provides for my family.

8. DETERMINATION IS A GIFT FROM GOD

Confidence in oneself can only begin from GOD. We need to understand that only his grace can allow us to live successfully. We are nothing without his spirit. So, if you think you are standing firm, be careful, so you don't fall! You need to see life from a new perspective. Nobody can help you if you are closed minded. Everything depends on your decisions, having determination to change your life and then leaping forward to start a new life.

Over the years, I have been fortunate enough to be introduced to so many people who were willing to provide me information that I needed in order to achieve what I ultimately wanted: FREEDOM. The ability to do what you want, when you want and with whom you want. I believe if you lived a holy life, you would never have the painful experiences of those who did not submit to GOD's ways.

After I became very spiritual and developed my very strong connection with GOD, he began to show me things. He steered me away from things that I didn't need to follow and thankfully he showed me people whom I definitely needed to begin following. I'm excited to say that I have been able to achieve many things in my life and there will be many more to come.

If you don't know my story, here goes. I started my own company 15 years ago, which allows me to do many things I really like such as traveling, spending time with my family and mentoring others who want to know how to do the same thing.

Just two summer ago, I decided to travel around the world. I spent a little over 40 days traveling from Washington DC to destinations such as Spain, France, Istanbul, Turkey and Israel. While traveling, I had a great time enjoying friends and it became one of the best months in my life. This was also the month which changed my life forever. I was immersed with vast learning about different cultures and different values from such incredible places around the world.

The only Reason this is Possible for me is because of the People who taught me ONE SKILL called "determination". Also, I think everything is in the hands of GOD. The power of GOD made this happen. God know everything because he knows us better than we know ourselves. Once you understand and Master this ONE SKILL, your life will never be the same.

He can perceive your thoughts from afar. He sees and knows the interior of your mind, He knows the thoughts that you never express. He knows not only what we do, but also why we do it. He knows not only where we go, but also how we get there. He knows not only who we know, but also how we know them. He knows not only what we said, but also how we say it. What I'm try to express in this book is that all good and bad in our life in known by GOD and can be achieved with the help of GOD.

STARTING A NEW LIFE FULL OF ENCOURAGEMENT

What I Did with GOD's purpose and More Importantly what is the reason to Do it became crystal clear to me! All you need to do is follow your inner voice, your spirit, and your dreams. If you will get in agreement with God, this is can be the greatest time of your life. With God on your side, you cannot possibly lose. He can open doors that no man can ever shut. He can cause you to be at the right place, at the right time. He can supernaturally turn your dreams into reality.

I know that I give thanks to GOD for my dreams coming true. My life is about enjoying the best of what life has to offer, while contributing great value to the world. I love helping the global community. This is my passion and dedication forever and always because GOD is going to honor my life and the life of my family.

If you want Freedom in Your Life as well, it is all about having a divine inspiration in your life and career. You can use the god given gift of determination to make your life as fruitful as possible. GOD wants you to be joyful and succeed. It is up to you to humbly accept this present and then do something with it.

9. YOU HAVE THE POWER TO DO GREAT THINGS

Now, don't make any excuses. Just take the first step on your path. The number one thing that holds most people back from ever taking action on their life's purpose is saying...<u>yes</u>! Everything depends on action and small choices.

Life starts to change in dynamic positive ways when you are committed towards something. You must pay the price and focus intently on reaching that goal. Handling your time with stern discipline is the key. When you have discipline, you will do the things that you should do which does include many things that you mostly don't like.

Remember, you have all the power you'll ever need to do whatever you want to do as long as you want it. Always be more than you think you are. Be brave. Be confident. But, more than anything, believe in you. Always, I will allow myself to be surprised by God. I will invite and welcome the miracles which are so effortless to the Divine Mind and see these come true.

I will be open to the greatness, generosity, and to the unparalleled imagination. I will respond with gratitude and dwell in the light of wonder. When you are grateful, you can see blessings flow in your life. Like many others, I believe that God brings many people in your life for a big purpose and to teach you something.

STARTING A NEW LIFE FULL OF ENCOURAGEMENT

Always, when their purpose is done, they vanish. The people that stay are there to remind you that loyalty and trust are the cornerstone of a great friendship.

Do not allow fear get to you. Panic can only hurt you. Worry can't undo us. When we exhale, we can hear You, oh Might GOD, warmly saying, "I am with you."

We hear GOD's message when he says, "There's no need to fear the big things, the little things, anything, for I'm your God. I will give you strength when the weight of it all wears you down, I will help you when you're hurting. I will hold you steady when everything wildly tilts. I will keep a grip on you so you can rest tonight, because you are held."

And all the people held on to each other because they belonged to each other and they all beheld a Grace that held them all. In the name of Jesus, the only One who ever loved us to death and back to the real and forever life, Amen.

SECTION II
<u>VALUES</u>

1. EXAMINE YOUR VALUES

You know, values are very important. I am privileged to be a woman who wins over any life challenges that come my way, especially the force of resistance. I built a reputation for excellence in intellectual motivation working with women. I was fruitful in using value driven lessons and encouragement to achieve notable results.

I'm constantly reminded that the manner in which we treat others, conduct ourselves and communicate during difficult times can alter the path of our lives and the lives of others. Your personal values are your roadmap for living a success life. The values will fully guide you through emotionally charged matters that transpire in your relationships. After all, any worthwhile relationship is based on trust and personalized attention.

For example: My family are elite attorneys in my origin country of Ecuador and they exhibit the highest level of professional values. They extrude excellence. The opportunity to work side by side with my family years ago was priceless. I felt very positive I could help my father's clients. It was also an incredible opportunity to assist them with reshaping their lives, especially by learning to respect their values.

It's important to examine what your values are before making a major decision such as starting a new life. Once you know what is most important to you, you can ensure that you make the right decisions to prioritize those values. Accepting who you are is the first step needed to making big changes.

Ask yourself some questions. For example, consider two people whom you admire. What do you most respect about them. Why? How could this play into your own life? For me, I respect GOD immensely. Any human can see that I fill my heart with love for him and GOD provides the supernatural support in my life.

Another good question to ask is what issues make you feel most inspired when you hear them talked about. For example, do you feel passionate about hearing about new inventions and wish you could be a part of that innovation process. See yourself strong like a rock, whereby you see yourself change from something weak to something productive and powerful. Maybe, it makes you feel fired up hearing about community service projects?

Examining this could help you figure out what you value most, such as innovation, ambition, social justice, or service. Remember that there are no "inferior" or "superior" personal values. One person might value adaptability, while someone else might value stability more highly. Neither is "wrong." It's all about embracing who you are and living a life that is in line with that.

You can find lists of core values online, if you need some help coming up with words to define them. Studies suggest that in general, people tend to place a very high value on their social relationships. These same people feel value and respect at their work. If one of these areas is lacking, you might consider focusing your "new life" efforts on that area.

STARTING A NEW LIFE FULL OF ENCOURAGEMENT

Remember, live in the present moment. You can't think yourself into a new way of acting. But you can act yourself into a new way of thinking. Most people try to think their way into a new mindset and then hope that their behavior will change. A better approach is to behave your way into a new mindset. When you start acting differently, you build a new frame of reference, and your thinking will follow.

Know that God is at work in our lives and he provided us so many values. Even when we can't see Him, He knows the ending of everyone's story before the beginning. I have learned to trust what I cannot see and feel. GOD wants us to trust Him. Our obedience to him is about the advancement of the kingdom of GOD.

2. BE HONEST

Lying violates trust and destroys relationships. Instead of lying, just be honest with those around you. Good people are honest and direct with what they're feeling and thinking. Talk to those people who are bothering you, instead of lying or getting others involved. Don't be passive-aggressive. Have integrity. Make your word mean something. If you say you are going to do something, then follow through on that promise. If circumstances arise that make it so you can't do it, be honest and direct to let the person know what happened.

Being honest doesn't mean being rude or cruel. Something new is always ahead of us. Unexpected beginnings can be the start of something grand. Good things are coming your way because God has a wonderful plan for your life and gives purpose for every challenge you face. Also you must take responsibility for your mistakes. This shows integrity, courage, and empathy. These are valuable traits to embrace and exhibit.

Remember that the 2 most powerful weapons in the battle to be your best are

1) your mind

2) how you think.

STARTING A NEW LIFE FULL OF ENCOURAGEMENT

This means you must persevere through difficult times in your life. Challenges are one of your toughest opponent. Winning isn't everything, it's the only thing. Challenges will mess with your head. That's right; they aim to take out your most powerful weapons before the battle even begins. Yes, I'm speaking of the battle of the mind.

As you move to a new version of yourself, get your mind right beginning now. You have to want to be successful and get better in anything you do in your life. You have to be determined. For example, I have spent so many hours at the court house helping many people on their cases. This time was full of practicing and practices to do my best. It means I never gave up, yet kept getting better with experience.

I wanted to do my best to protect and defend my clients. It means when you miss your chance or make a bad decision, you choose to come back even stronger. You know internally that in order to succeed, you must first fail.

You must also think big and see yourself as being the best at whatever you do. Donald Trump once said: "I like thinking big. If you are going to be thinking anyway, you might as well think big." I also liked what great basketball player Tim Duncan once said: "Good, better, best. Never let it rest. That is what I have learned from my coach and I will never forget his words."

I want to be the best self I can be. I want to go far in my life and be successful. I have goals. Only with hard work, determination and perseverance I can do all I dream and more.

3. BE EDUCATED

Grow up and step into being the Woman That "YOU" Want to <u>BE</u>. Stop picturing yourself somewhere else. Don't procrastinate, and then not go for it. What the heck good is that? There is a life to be lived. There are many opportunities out there. Educate yourself. Make a point to build yourself with different types of perspectives. Never compromise following your dreams. You must develop your best potential. Find encouraging information, such as this book, that will train you to start operating your life independently.

All of the information you can obtain will be a great resource to help guide you. You have in your hands material to create a strong foundation for your future changes. If you start little by little, you will see steady progress. Incorporate new perceptions into your daily life because once you unlock the various mysteries about yourself, you will discover the new "YOU" is unstoppable.

As a CEO, I served the community well, and growing it is very important. I too, knew I need to become educated. I have always given an important role in my life for study. I think education gives you the knowledge, skills, and credibility to achieve your maximum potential. In terms of financial success, statistics have shown that the more education you have, the higher degree you will achieve; therefore, the more money you are likely to make

4. LIVE PURPOSEFULLY

Respect your time and where you put your attention. Decide what will be your chosen path and style of action. Some people use their intelligence to pursue writing activities, while others become skilled in sculpting, mathematics or countless other activities. Examine your likes and dislikes. Decide for yourself how you want to bring to life your personal life vision.

None are any less important or superior than the other; what matters is the direction in which you go. Examine your chosen field of talent or passion and match it will suitable action. To achieve your dreams and be the person that you want to be, you need to start paying attention to your actions. Please ask yourself, "What I'm doing going to lead me to where I want to be in life?"

You probably feel disconnected from what you're doing if:

1) You find yourself constantly bored, daydreaming about the future /past or counting down the minutes until the day ends

2) You are tired of asking GOD for HELP; thereby you forget to create a connection and bow to him, revering that he is in control of our life.

But remember you have many amazing dreams inside you. In order to be happy, let God do his job; thus you will realize everything that's possible in your life. Many options are available in life for you just one step at the time. Sometimes it's important to consider changing your career to a field that you care about. Do not forget that it could also mean there needs to be changes you are not thinking of yet.

Does that job you are pursuing pay enough to support your lifestyle? Is it something you might get bored of eventually? Do you really want to commit to that job? Cherish your time. Try to spend your free time doing things that you enjoy doing, rather than wasting time. For example, rather than spending your weekends watching television, week after week, spend them partaking in hobbies that excite you or spend time with loved ones.

Keep in mind that the concept of "wasted time" is relative. Not everything you do has to be productive in the conventional sense. It should be engaging. With enjoyable activities in your life, there will be a spark of energy to move forward into the change you seek. I have always have said, "God, I trust in you and my future is in your hands!"

5. BE HEALTHY

Your body is your vehicle to everything you achieve. Such physical activity doesn't only keep the body physically healthy; it also improves one's mental state.

Successful people think differently, act differently and ultimately distinguish themselves from unsuccessful people by taking a distinctive path toward their goals.

Set regular health activities to keep you healthy. For instance, Ex-president of the United States of America, Barack Obama exercises 45 minutes per day, six days a week.

Many busy moms and dads across the world, in spite of their hectic schedules, also still find the time to hit the gym, do yoga or some other fitness type of activity. If they can make it happen, there is no reason you should not do the same for your own health.

6. BE YOURSELF

I want to reflect about myself and how I followed my dream. Entrepreneurship allowed me to do work that was engaging and empowering. So, what is it that holds more women back from taking the plunge? Sometimes, a "good enough" life in itself becomes a deterrent.

College, the corporate ladder, a family; quite often, these things feel comfortable. "I was successful at a job that I wasn't really happy at" is what some people are secretly feeling. Change is what is needed.

Being the CEO of my own venture was a new reality I chose; the path of being an entrepreneur. I wanted everything set up perfectly. I wanted to share the same formula for success I used in my past work.

But there's no magic formula for entrepreneurial success, of course. Stepping into the unknown is scary -- and many people doubt their abilities, feeling like impostors. I believe that no matter how thoroughly in fear a woman might be, you can create your successful future.

As a Women and CEO, I remember hesitating early on to pursue entrepreneurship, all stemming from fear of not having enough time for me and my family. But I say the biggest challenge is balancing the running of my business with running my household. It's a challenge and I realize nothing is impossible for me.

STARTING A NEW LIFE FULL OF ENCOURAGEMENT

Sometimes, I say my home is my office, making it that much tougher to get work done. My kids and home create comfort and distractions. It's a balance here. Just remember, you can change your world if you want start from you. Remember to be yourself always and never be who you're not.

Don't try to be like somebody else; just be yourself and do good things as simply as you can. Being yourself helps you be a genuine person who can reflect positivity into the world. Staying true to yourself helps you find focus and understand your core values and what you find important.

Share your possessions, your positivity, and your happiness. Don't be emotionally stingy. Be generous and encouraging. Share your knowledge. Share opportunities. Share your time. Share your food with others. Never take the biggest slice of pizza or piece of meat.

No two people are exactly alike. It's fine to feel shy about a talent, hobby or even your personality. Lots of people feel that way. Using your imagination can help you become less timid. Express yourself to other people and they will most likely accept you for who you are; especially when they see how genuine you are.

7. BE HUMBLE: THE UNIVERSE DOES NOT REVOLVE AROUND YOU

Every day I count my blessings. Some examples of blessings might be: a new day, a warm bed, a loving spouse, a child in your life, a unique personality, or a special talent. You have wonderful things in your life already. Gratitude quickly sets in when we begin to spend a quiet moment each day remembering them.

This practice alone has the potential to change your heart and life immeasurably. Stop focusing on what you don't have. Too many people never realize gratitude because they spend so much mental energy focused on what they don't have. Throw away catalogs and advertisements that inevitably promise you more fulfillment and joy in life.

Those things are not sold in stores. They never have been, and never will be. Go take a walk in the park. Stand near the bottom of a waterfall. Look at the world from the top of a mountain. Go for a long hike. Swim in an ocean. Find your own way of being in nature and take the time to truly appreciate all that it entails. Close your eyes and feel the breeze on your face.

You should feel completely humbled by nature; a force that is so immense in its depth and power. As you develop your wonder and respect for all of the things that were there long before you were and which will be there long after you are gone, you will begin to realize just how small you are in this world.

Spending more time in nature will make you see how big and complicated the world is and that you're not at the center of it. To start a new life, you need to ask the right questions. Start with these: **1)** Am I helping and inspiring other people more and more every day. **2)** Am I having a great family life with incredible friendships around me?

This is priceless. If you think your life need some improvement, I suggest to do something new that you have never done before. Please don't think negative thoughts, because these can destroy your life. Once you start thinking positive, an incredible thing can happen in your life. Act with confidence and think about something beautiful. Smiling is contagious to the other people around you and you can start helping other people with your positive attitude.

You can create new goals. I've provided several positive thinking strategies to help you overcome negative patterns that have prevented you from achieving your goals in the past. Choose several you feel will help you most and incorporate them into your daily life. A great example is how powerful you feel once you can learn not to apologize or accepting blame for someone else's anger.

Write down these strategies and remind yourself to pause and change your way of thinking each time you find yourself being critical of yourself. You will become more comfortable with each new way of thinking. Give yourself time and be kind to yourself as you are progressively developing into the new you.

8. CHECK IN WITH YOURSELF

When people attempt to put you down, don't talk back or take it to heart. Instead, laugh or shrug it off, or simply say you're sorry they feel this way. This will show you are too smart to sink down to their level and will prevent you from being harsh, aggressive, and a bad person.

Not to mention, when they see how well you handle the situation, even your aggressors may back off or lose their interest in insulting you. Don't downplay or sidestep expressions of affection or honor from others. The ability to accept or receive is a universal mark of an individual with solid self-esteem.

Be fair to all people. Treat everyone with kindness, and do not be mean or rude to people, even if they don't agree with you. Do not bully. Instead, stand up for the bullied. Don't talk about others behind their backs.

Be a genuine person. If you have a problem with someone, confront them in a respectful way. Don't spread bad things about them when they are not around. Don't unfairly judge people. You don't know the circumstances surrounding them. Give people the benefit of the doubt, and respect their choices.

Treat others the way you'd like to be treated. Remember the golden rule. Put the energy out into the universe you'd like to receive. Respect extends to your surroundings, too. Don't throw trash on the floor. Don't purposefully mess up things, and don't talk too loud with obnoxious type of behavior. Respect that other people share the same space as you.

9. TAKE YOUR TIME

Don't be in a hurry in life. Slow down and enjoy the simple things. I often see that some of my clients are competitive people who just want to win. However, focusing on other things always is the best way to get you there. If you only obsess about the win, it's very stressful and can take you out of your mental game. I know the pressure to make a prompt solution can overwhelm you. Please don't focus on the process and choose to let the outcome take care of itself.

Time is a medium that helps us organize our days. Sometimes you have to follow the timetable, like when you're on your way to work or getting your kids to school. You must learn to accept the natural stress of the process. Better yet, of course, if you have no time commitments. Either way, learn to live in the moment.

Be patient with people. Think the best about them instead of the worst. Don't think that the person who almost cut you off while driving on the road is a jerk; instead, understand that she or he may be late for work or to pick up their child. Don't be in a hurry to get to the store and get back. Enjoy the scenery as you pass by. While in the store, notice all the fine and colorful fruits and vegetables that are there for your nourishment, and realize that others are not as fortunate to enjoy the same benefit.

STARTING A NEW LIFE FULL OF ENCOURAGEMENT

You must learn to accept the natural stress and use that stressful energy as a calming mechanism. It's a strange phenomenon, but it's true. Once your train your brain how to react to the stress and change with a smile, a deep breath, a head nod or even a gentle body sway, your body will begin to associate that type of stress to that of relaxation.

With consistent practice your body will soon begin to respond automatically and you won't even think twice about it. Always, I think anger only begets anger. Now remember your opponent is not always a living breathing person. Your problems can come in various ways. It's important to get your mind right. This is no easy task.

You must invest time, energy and consistent effort to find what works for you, but once you do it, it's done. Enjoy your time when you focus on helping others. For example: Buy some extra nourishing food to give to the food bank to help feed others. Suggest to the manager of a grocery store that they should have food sold at a discount and put a food drop off location somewhere in the store for the purpose of feeding the poor.

Only use the car horn in an emergency situation. Don't blow it at a little old man that can barely see over the wheel or someone driving extremely slowly. Realize that driver may be taking his time so he doesn't injure himself or someone else. If they rush past you, like I already mentioned, understand that they may be in a hurry for something important. Even if they are not, why add to already negative feelings.

10. BE SOLUTION ORIENTATED

Always think about creating solutions. Stay away from framing experiences as problems. One of the things that impresses me the most is when we experience life transitions. For example, if your family is moving away to a new state/province, don't be sad for the change. Think that this change happened for some good reason even if you cannot see it at the moment.

Be happy for your family because they have chosen a certain change which is beneficial to them. This change on some level allows them to feel that they also are getting a fresh start on life. Let them have their cake and eat it too, instead of spoiling the joy for them. Celebrate this joy with them.

For example: my parents provided the foundation that enabled me to ultimately achieve victory in my life. I'm determined to honor them by helping those women victimized in my community who are struggling with domestic violence. I know that their voices are being heard. They are such valuable human beings, and each of these women have great futures ahead of them.

When I moved to the USA I started earning credits from the College of Frederick and after that from the University of Maryland. I graduated and then received my degree in Law. It truly shaped me into a hard-working, conscientious student with a desire to learn more and more. God has giving me the tools to be a person with a strong foundation and big ambition for the future.

Examples of this include:

1) working in my own companies

2) working diligently to be a great leader that helps so many families.

These positive interactions in my life have exhibited a genuine illustration about me. Some people have described me using very powerful valedictorian level words. Others have chosen much humbler, simple words. Either way, I have received these utterances with preserved kindness and innocence. I keep immense appreciation for their kindness.

God always gives me the tools to succeed in my life. Also, it's important to have enough wisdom to discern success. I enjoy literature, particularly British, including the plays of William Shakespeare. I like how his work is very complex, and it's hard to understand at times. Yet, it is good, and incredibly delightful. It inspires me with my own abilities to affect positive results towards people's drama filled lives.

My objective is to accomplish building a culture of peace. It contains certain aspects such as music, community, youth empowerment and coalition building to make everyone feel alive again. This was the atmosphere that pervaded during the 1st Annual International Conference we held for my non-profit organization.

With over 250 attendees from 8 countries and 14 states, the goal was to share wisdom, culture, commonality and purpose. This was brilliantly put forward in a way that combined activism with art, music culture and education to get across the message of unity in action and community without violence.

11. SAY YES TO STARTING A NEW LIFE

As a humble person, you should recognize that everyone, including you, has their own goals and dreams. Each person may want to talk about their achievements and their opinions on things. One of the major impediments to discovering your purpose is the money excuse. You buy into the lie that it's impossible to make money doing what you love.

So, you don't even bother to search for your purpose. The first step is to find your purpose, then later you can find a way to make money doing it. For instance, Volunteer in your community. Choose to volunteer for something you find really interesting. High quality people like to volunteer. They are nice, giving, and enjoy meeting new people.

Not only will you get to be around great people, but you also might happen to discover your purpose along the way. it simply means acknowledging that, as human beings, none of us are perfect and none of us can do everything by ourselves. Humble people don't have to be meek wallflowers. Being humble doesn't mean not having any self-esteem.

However, a humble person should be mindful of everyone in the conversation and shouldn't talk down or disrupt anyone. A big part of being humble is respecting others, and part of respecting others is helping them. Treat other people as equals, and help them because it is the right thing to do. It's been said that when you can help others who cannot possibly help you in return, you have learned humility.

Helping people in need will also make you appreciate what you have even more. Similarly, find a mentor for you too. Find people you aspire to be like in certain areas, and ask them to mentor you. Mentorship requires good boundary setting, confidentiality and discernment.

Remain humble and teachable. As soon as you cross the line of being unteachable, bring yourself back down to earth again. Being teachable means that you admit that you always have more to learn about life.

You can be humbler by taking classes in something you know nothing about, such as pottery or screen writing, and knowing that you will let others teach you and show you the way. This can help you realize that everyone is good at different things. We all need to help each other in order to become better people.

SECTION III
<u>MINDSET</u>

1. BE DETERMINED TO FOLLOW A NEW DESTINY

There is something extraordinary inside of you. Believe you are not an average person. You need to think carefully and put in place some plan of action strategies, designed to achieve a major overhaul in your life. And because you are under pressure to make this happen sooner rather than later, you will become a spectacular human being in the process.

GOD can see your pure heart which resides inside each and every one of us. Recognize what is inside of you to determine why you feel the need to start a new life. Remember, no one can be you. You must overcome your own internal and external challenges as you pursue this path.

Don't live in the past. Today is a new opportunity to conquer the world. For example, think like today is your birthday with many new opportunities, new challenges and new adventures waiting to happen. Think that each year is a new opportunity for you. Think that you are special and have great potential.

So many people miss the big opportunities in their life because they get comfortable in that restrictive box called "zone of comfort". Don't let these opportunities pass. You need to desire accomplishing goals. Don't miss your moment. Many blessings are waiting for you. It is just up to you to take advantage of them.

STARTING A NEW LIFE FULL OF ENCOURAGEMENT

A great example is if you're a new empty-nester facing life without kids in the house for the first time in decades, you might think appropriately it's time to start a new stage of your life. After all, you aren't a primary caretaker for your children anymore and can reframe your life to focus more on you. Don't miss this moment for creating a new you.

On the other hand, don't miss your moment using a life change to escape unpleasant feelings, as that isn't a good idea, since this avoidance doesn't address taking care of yourself, no matter where you are in the journey.

The real issues you may be experiencing, along with the emotions, will tend to follow you wherever you go. You have to deal with them before you can truly start a fresh life. Always be determined to fulfill your new life purpose. Be conscious that this new destiny is full of much potential and encouragement.

2. YOU MUST LOVE THE NEW YOU

Don't let people tell you they hate the new you, unless you care about their opinion over your own. Even if it was your mother or best friend, you must fall in the love with the new you for your reasons, not theirs.

Successful people all have similar traits and similar patterns. The truth is that being successful is not far-fetched if you can learn what other successful people do. And no, it doesn't have to be big acts of philanthropy or innovation. It can be small things; things you can do every day to reach the new you.

Be yourself; Stay in character of who you are. Don't change because someone wants you to. Don't change if you don't feel comfortable being something different. Be sure you're always comfortable in your body. If someone insults you, don't insult them back. Just laugh and walk away. Always practice positive self-talk.

When you use phrases like, "today is going to be a great day" or "I am successful", you boost your intellectual ability and improve your chances of attaining your goals for the day. If it's hard to change your attitude, pretend you're in a drama club or an improvisation club, and make believe that the person you're trying to be is your character. You need to learn to be like them in order to be successful in the play. The same is true in life.

3. THINK BEFORE YOU JUDGE OTHERS

Think before you approach to judge a person. Then I say please, chose not to hate the bad ones. Sometimes people are not bad. They are just not educated enough to distinguish right from wrong. You have to remember this in order to learn and become wiser.

Love is a unique feeling. Love is patient, kind and without envy. It's not rude, and it keeps no record of wrong. Love is pure when you give it to someone who deserves it. Don't be afraid to make mistakes. Part of being humble is understanding that you will make mistakes. That is only natural.

Know that everyone else will make mistakes too, and you will have a heavy burden lifted off of you. However, this doesn't mean that you should be sloppy. Try to avoid obvious mistakes, but don't be afraid to try new methods or ways of accomplishing your goals.

Each person can only experience a tiny sliver of life at a time. There will always be people who are older and wiser than you. Your elders' opinions could be worth listening to, although you must make the decision based on your knowledge of them.

4. AVOID ABSOLUTES AND EXAGGERATIONS

Different strategies can help you to achieve the long-term objectives of your life. Giving praise will also encourage others to praise you, and this builds up your confidence to continue on the path. At all costs, be sure to avoid absolutes and exaggerations. Correct your internal voice when it exaggerates, especially when it exaggerates the negative thoughts. For example, "I always eat too much" or "I'll never lost weight".

Absolutes means that a statement is always 100 percent true, but there are very few absolutes in life. If you exaggerate or use an absolute, rephrase what you say instead. For example, "I always eat too much" can be changed to, "In the past, I've often eaten too much. Now, I'm getting better at how much I eat." Then feel good about taking control of your thoughts. Halt negative thoughts immediately.

Sometimes putting a stop to negative thinking is as easy as that. The next time you start giving yourself an internal critique session, tell yourself to stop it. If you saw a person yelling insults at someone else, you'd probably tell them to stop, wouldn't you. Why do you accept that behavior from yourself? Look for the positive. Did you know that love is a word derived from the Sanskrit word that means looking for the good?

STARTING A NEW LIFE FULL OF ENCOURAGEMENT

Be loving toward yourself and others, and instead of focusing on what you think your negative qualities are, accentuate your strengths and assets. Maybe you didn't develop enough stamina this month to run a mile, but perhaps your hard work and perseverance led to losing an additional five pounds. Maybe you felt nervous and self-conscious when going out to a formal social event, but you received numerous comments from friends that they were happy you joined them and had a good time. It's OK to blow it. That is all part of life and the learning process.

Maybe you got so nervous and embarrassed that you couldn't keep up in fitness class or felt bad that you gave in and ate those potato chips. It's OK. All people have weaknesses, and we all fall off the path at times or don't do things as well as we think we should. Your boss, coworkers, friends, family, governor and favorite movie stars have all had embarrassing moments and setbacks.

Perfection is a high goal, yet don't start or even end there. Make doing your best into your ideal goal. Focus on what you've gained from the process and how you can use it in the future. Avoid focusing on what wasn't done or should have been done differently.

Allow yourself to make mistakes and then forgive yourself. Compliment yourself and others around you on your achievements. For Example, I have always said, "Well, we may not have done it all, but we did a pretty great job with what we did."

5. BE A MAN'S DREAM WOMAN

Be confident and unstoppable. Nothing more. Why? Because then you will stand for something, and have the confidence to back it up. You will expect and even require more from others, because you now expect and deliver more from yourself. You will quickly realize that you have been settling for crumbs and selling yourself short.

You deserve more than that. And the second that you realize that, you will GET better than that. Because you won't accept less than you deserve. But it all starts with you. Be the example of your expectation of others. Ask yourself these questions:

1) Am I experiencing the <u>Happiness</u> I truly want and deserve on a daily basis?

2) Am I attracting the <u>Wealth</u> I truly want and deserve in my life?

Once you have a purpose, and you act on your purpose, then your needs will be met and you will be showing your worth. Then others will treat you as if you are worthy. It takes courage. The root of courage is having a solid core inside of you to build from. Courage isn't about going off to war, saving a family from a burning home, putting yourself in the line of fire, or doing superhuman tasks.

Courage is simply about being true to your core. That can be scary for many because that requires vulnerability. It takes courage to tap into your stripped down, raw self, and then act on it. It takes courage to be you without fear of judgment, hurt, or failure. A confident woman knows her worth. She takes pride in herself, which is apparent through her attitude and appearance.

She isn't looking for approval from guys. She knows she's pretty great. She also knows that the right guy will be very lucky to be with her because she has the ability to make him happier than any other woman can. Fact is, guys want to feel like they won the prize, like they are dating the head of the cheer leading team.

They want to feel like they are the luckiest guy in the room. Just as he wants you to be proud of him, he wants to be proud of you. If you carry around a bummer, insecure, self-deprecating, "I'm not so great" attitude, then why would he feel like he scored by having you in his life? Whether it's your looks, smarts, triumphs, the respect you garner, your career, or simply how you push yourself through pain points and get out of box, he wants to feel like he can show you off.

He needs to know that he can confidently "bring you home to mom", introduce you to his friends, and accompany him to business dinners with his boss; all because you make him look good. Do you have integrity, and the strength to act on it? Are you strong in your values and beliefs? Or do you waver, fluctuate, appear wishy washy or easily influenced.

Who are you? What do you believe in? Do you stand by it? Do you have integrity or are your words and beliefs worthless? Can he depend on what you say? Do your actions align with your words? A woman who has unshakable beliefs, who shows and tells the same story, is someone who makes a man feel safe.

A feeling of safety is one of the most crucial elements when it comes to a man's ability to trust, let his guard down, and open his heart completely. He knows that he can depend on you for good or for bad, in sickness and in health, weakness and triumph. In moments of uncertainty, the one thing that he can be certain of is you, because you are certain of you. Do you do that? If not, then you should!

6. LOVE YOURSELF

My dad used to say that no matter how good or bad you have it, there's always someone who has it better than you and someone who has it worse than you. Comparison is the root of despair. Every day, we get to choose to be grateful for what we have, regardless of where we want to be.

Gratitude really matters. A grateful heart is a contented heart. A contented heart is a simple heart. And a simple heart leads to a simplified life. Decide to Go Last for a change. If you're always rushing to get things done first and get to the front of the line, challenge yourself to allow others to go before you.

For example, elders, disabled people, children, or people in a hurry. Ask yourself, "Do I really need to do this first so badly?" The answer will almost always be NO! Learn to love yourself in every way. Practice unconditional, self-acceptance. The only way you can truly love others is to first have confidence and love yourself.

What you do and what you believe must make you feel good as well as others. If you try to do things for others without taking care of yourself, you can end up resentful, angry, and negative. If you love yourself, then you will make a positive impact when you help others.

Are you superficially acting like a good person? If you are self-loathing and angry on the inside, you may not be a good person despite all your outward actions. Don't bully yourself! Don't hold yourself to standards that you wouldn't expect others to meet. It's great to want to do well, but expecting yourself to be better than the best and then punishing yourself when you fail is a vicious cycle.

Using expressions like "I should have" is just a way of punishing yourself, after the fact. Stop it! Live in the present and move forward. Don't drag the past along for the ride; it gets very heavy. Do you remember the children's story of the little train that could? That's how you need to live your life. Keep saying to yourself, "I know I can."

Tell your subconscious you've already done it. Be kind to yourself and remember you can do this. Encourage yourself. Instead of focusing on the negative. Replace your criticism with encouragement. Give constructive suggestions instead of being critical. "Maybe if I try to do it again next time, it would be even better," instead of "I didn't do that right."

7. PRACTICE DEVELOPING MINDFULNESS

Prove it to yourself, yet not feel an obligation to provide it to anyone else. You can grow your strategies by developing specific behaviors and then follow through with careful repetitive practice. Yes, there are so many different elements of concentration.

For example: All of us are very hard on ourselves. If you have a great week and then a bad week, probably you think about your bad week first, but everyone here knows we are capable of doing great things. It's just a matter of doing it and also not putting all your focus and emphasis on what went wrong.

I have had certain epiphany behavior changes too. There was one time when I had not been doing exercise for long time. On a particular night, there was this sudden motivation that came from inside of me. I felt this willingness to change my body shape. I instantly decided that every morning I would wake up at 5 am. At the beginning, I felt exhausted with the new routine, but once I got into that gym environment and worked out well, I loved it, especially when the new "ME" appeared.

I actually had to change my behavior in order to have a great body. When you perform like I did, it's something that's always a part of you. To get results, you must use a repertoire of behaviors and practices that, through repetition and perseverance.

Develop laser focus on what you want and intensify that concentration. Creating new strategies and welcoming new information do make a huge difference. Through practice, we can help perfect these behaviors and increase our concentration so that we can leverage all the new information we acquire.

Always remain open minded to new information and stop taking a single narrow viewed perspective. You must break the old patterns. Remember, part of welcoming new information is to ask powerful questions. Learn to appreciate the inquiry process. This substantially removes your blind spots and assists in adopting more than one view point. Learn as well via active listening and opinion swap with other people.

Time is your most limited and precious resource. What's the best thing you should be thinking about? This is about asking whether the problem you have now is even worth your time. Before you throw all of you into it, figure out whether it's worth it. Is it significant? Please think how much time you should spend on it. Sometimes, the situation may not be urgent enough to put your attention to right now. You can always revisit it later.

Focus less on emotional reactions and be more driven by intelligent interaction. This means that you should start thinking about a problem before choosing how you want to proceed. Do not just rush to conclusions or ride an emotional roller coaster. Do not fall for the trap of getting lost in the details of the problem either.

Rather than reacting impulsively, step back, consider how you want to approach and then move forward with confidence.

Play with possibilities, including viewing the various layers of what is involved. Realize that some challenges may even need longer time frames to resolve such as one to five years. Consider evaluating strengths and weaknesses of the components as well as to the way you would choose to handle them.

The good news is this: thinking is a good skill and there are plenty of resources that we can use to improve our thinking techniques. Let's focus to encourage developing our self from the inside with a different mentality. We need to change the average thinking by starting to see ourselves as doing more, and get our enjoyment back. Find the right direction in your life. Raising your self-esteem is a gradual process that does not happen in one instant.

Self-esteem is an indication of how we feel and how we think about ourselves. This creates a conviction of what we believe we can or cannot do. I believe that anything can happen in your life when you work with tenacity and integrity. Self-esteem can be measured by how we act. However, it is not a permanently fixed state. It changes in relation to the experiences we have and our current state of feelings.

Self-esteem can rise, but this does not happen overnight, nor by a twist of fate. It is achieved through a conscientious and persistent process. Remember, everything you need is within you. You are powerful beyond all measure. It is about changing your attitude. Give yourself a good self-complement every single day!

8. STAY POSITIVE

How you talk to yourself is very important, and it can be the key to your self-esteem. Regardless of the messages you received from others while growing up, and regardless of what you hear from others in your life now, what's most important is how you feel about yourself.

You can insulate yourself from the criticism of others by taking good care of your own self-image. So I urge you to <u>Compliment Yourself</u>! Start to do this, every single day.

And not just once! You can set an alert on your phone for every hour, and when it goes off compliment yourself! Or you can plan to compliment yourself every time you go by a mirror, or before and after each meal, or whatever intervals you think you can remember.

It may sound too simple to work, but the reality is that the more you crowd your brain with positive thoughts about yourself, the more you push out negative ones. And, the more you bolster yourself, the more resistant you are to self-doubt and also to the criticisms of others. It doesn't matter what the compliment is. It's the act itself that matters.

When you give yourself a compliment, you are actively examining your strengths, which can increase both your sleek and self-confidence. Over the course of the day, you'll realize your focus is on your strengths and positive traits. You won't be spending time dwelling on the things you like less about yourself.

You'll get other benefits from self-complimenting too. For one thing, your day will be punctuated with little self-confidence boosts, you will find yourself complimenting other people more, thus making them feel good about themselves. You will probably become more positive because you have shifted your center of attention to noticing positive things.

You might even find that you stand up a little straighter, become more confident, and attract more positive energy your way. Those are a lot of benefits from a few acts requiring little effort, wouldn't you say. Give it a try. Here are some ideas to get you started. Self-Compliments. Where to Start? Your self-compliments can be big or small, but don't put too much pressure on yourself to say something momentous each time.

Big Compliments might be: "I love my eyes/smile/freckles" or anything else you love about physical yourself. "I am beautiful inside and out. I'm a great conversationalist, even with the people I don't know. "

The Little Things Count such as: "I love my laugh. I did a great job getting everyone to school and work on time today. I'm a better golfer than any of my golfing buddies. I showed interminable patience with that telemarketer today. That was the best meal I cooked all week. "

Fun Compliments might be: "My hair looks so shiny today. I tell the best jokes. These shoes make my calves look awesome." I hope you'll have fun giving yourself compliments.

Give yourself a bunch of self-compliments and see how you feel. No matter what happened in your life each step leads to success because you are an amazing human being so lovely and caring, talented in so many ways, with an indomitable spirit, a laugh out loud sense of humor, and an incomparable zest for life, you're one of a kind.

9. PROCEED WITH A WINNING ATTITUDE AND POSITIVE APTITUDE

These 2 quotes are some of my all-time favorites.

"Never let it rest. Until your good is better and your better is best."

-Tim Duncan

"You have a winning and valuable attitude because you are so Valuable"

-Unknown

Few people have experience with intentional, focused thinking. We spend very little time thinking about what we are thinking about. For most, thinking is a poorly development ability that often occurs with little conscious awareness.

We can probably go through hours of activities a day without giving any notice to the quality of our thoughts passing through our mind. Our thinking becomes more like background noise while we engage in activities. Yet behind everything we do is a thought, and each individual thought intrinsically contributes to our overall character. Become the best with a positive attitude. This is far more important than out aptitude alone.

Some People continually cultivate a positive attitude because they are more inclined to expect great things and are more likely to achieve them. Some People are so optimistic and generally happier, healthier, and more successful than those with a negative outlook. Developing a positive winning attitude takes some work. The received benefits are obvious, although you'll work harder at what you do, but it will be easier to get others to help you achieve your dreams and goals.

Thinking positive also encourages stronger and more productive relationships which lead to greater success at work and at home. Here are some things you can do daily to develop a positive outlook on life. Become the best with a winning attitude. For example, a long time ago, I had a big important charity event for my not-profit organization. That day I felt intimidated because I knew that more than 300 people will be there in attendance.

That day, for some reason, I heard the song, called 'BELIEVE IN YOURSELF' (The Wiz) play in my mind. It's a great song about believing in yourself, in your heart. That song inspired me and eased my fear. That day was so important because

1) Telemundo Network was hosting the event

2) I had to make a speech.

That night my heart was pounding so fast. Somehow though, when I was present in front of so many people, my winning attitude took hold. All the people were surprised by my speech and indeed stood up to congratulate me with so much applause. That was so inspiring to me, as I witnessed so many people believing in me, all in one location.

That support was so important. Because I felt it was my time. For that moment, I was the queen of my own destiny. Always, I think positive things at every opportunity during my day. These positive thoughts can change our day more than anything else in this world. It is like a magnet to bring positive events into our life.

Don't rush yourself. Get up on time and get ready for your new day in a relaxed mood. If you are late, you only complicate your day by making yourself feel unorganized. It's important that you have prepared your agenda with anticipation for your activities. Use positive upbeat music to allow yourself to wake up early with joy in your life.

Remember the whole idea is to start your day with a positive attitude. Waking up early is very uplifting step that will you enable you to approach day by day with a positive attitude. Make sure you eat a healthy breakfast. A good breakfast can give you the energy that you need to face the new day. Breakfast is one of the most important meals of the day. Holding a winning aptitude in life can attract golden opportunities to eventually come along.

Of course, it is important for people to have skills, training and experience, but I have always been a huge believer in putting attitude above aptitude. You can come fully equipped for a role, but without real enthusiasm, the best skill-set will count for very little. You can train somebody and give them the tools, but you can't give them the right attitude. They either possess it or they do not.

The key to real success is an ability to adapt to change. That will never happen if you approach challenge with a negative attitude. People with the right mental attitude can always take something positive from a difficult situation. Most importantly, be constantly looking at ways of moving life on to the next stage of its journey.

10. USE POSITIVE THINKING AND PROJECT YOUR MENTAL GIANT

Bring a positive attitude to every situation. Think about a time when you were victorious. For example, I remember when I ran the entire 5K marathon. I saw myself there with my friends. Yes, it was an amazing experience. But what got me through was that mental image. That is your mental giant and now it's time for you to introduce that giant to the world.

It is incredible to see yourself in Victory. Standing tall, being powerful, and exuding the character of a true winner. When you process pain in a negative manner, it only hurts yourself and others. No matter what you experience, if you react negative as a response, it has a direct harmful impact on the way you treat others.

Counselors can't make the pain go away, but they provide some important strategies to help the process of this experience be digested in a healthy way. Unfortunately, our mentality can influence the achievements of our days. If something doesn't turn out your way, try to change what you can. Choose to smile, stay positive, and move on. Just don't choose to get stuck on focusing on bad incidents that occurred in your life.

"It is better to light a single candle than it is to curse the darkness!"

-The Motto of the Christopher Society

For example: I remember the most painful time of my life when my father died and I needed to inform my family. I felt like something was dying inside me, and I had to suddenly become extremely strong. I needed to provide emotional support to my family and assist in hosting the funeral.

I needed to speak in front of hundreds of people, in spite of my own emotional overload. I looked at my notes and saw what appeared to be nothing; as if my mind was not there. My heart was beating ferociously and I saw all these faces looking at me. All I felt like doing was crying.

However, inside me, something was convincing me that I can do this. Obviously, the emotional collapse was a process for my evolution; the dynamics of processing pain made me a stronger woman that I could ever imagine that I could be. I have realized how transition leads to transformation.

When you see controversy, try to be the one who changes the subject by suggesting a solution. Don't state what you would do, but ask everyone to get involved. Transitions can also be very difficult, but remember no matter how painful it is, if we embrace the transition process, then we can experience transformation.

11. FAILURE IS NOT AN ENDING

View a misstep as the conclusion of one performance, not the end of your entire career. Refuse to see yourself as a failure, though you must own up to your shortcomings. A failure may be something you have done. It may even be something you'll have to do again on the way to success.

A failure is definitely not something you are. If you're at a point where you're feeling very negatively about yourself, be aware that you're now ideally positioned to make rapid and dramatic improvement. A negative self- evaluation, if it's honest and insightful, takes much more courage and character than the self-delusions that underlie arrogance and conceit.

I've seen the truth of this proven many times with athletes. After an extremely poor performance, a team or an individual athlete often does much better the next time out, especially when the poor performance was so bad that there was simply no way to shirk responsibility for it.

Disappointment, defeat, and even apparent failure are in no way permanent conditions, unless we choose to make them so. On the contrary, these undeniably painful experiences can be the solid foundation on which to build future success. When you realize that you cannot force someone into doing something, you give him or her freedom and allow them to experience the consequences.

In doing so, you find your own freedom as well. Once you get the point that it truly is impossible to please everyone, you begin to live purposefully. Daily, I know through prayer, things will happen, all in God's time. Once you place it in his hands, he will take care of your situation. My faith is strong and I'm so thankful for the awesome power of prayer.

A woman is unstoppable once she realizes that she deserves better. Can you loudly and firmly say the affirmation "my needs are valid." Do you believe it? Until you realize, accept, believe, and own that you are a high quality, worthy women, whose needs are valid and should be heard, no one else will believe it either. And when you do believe it, you'll be unstoppable.

But at first, if you're like most women, you have no idea. Isn't that sad. It is. It's sad that you don't know, that you haven't taken the time to listen to yourself, to tap into your core, to hear, and really listen to what you need. I'm not talking about what you need based on insecurity, self-doubt, anger, resentment, hurt, or an attempt to please another.

The way to really look at integrity is this: Do my feelings match my words and my actions? Is there a disconnect or a break within that statement. It's ok if there is. That's common. And that's exactly what you need to address.

12. PUSH PAST YOUR COMFORT ZONE

Staying in your comfort zone is a quick path to going nowhere. All people who increased their enjoyment in life, and were more successful chose to challenge themselves with new uncomfortable situations. Yes, it can make you feel nervous to be out of your comfort zone, however, the magic all happens once you do step into this unchartered territory.

Pushing past your comfort zone has been proven to improve your performance and increase your likelihood of finding success. Please focus your attention on meeting your objectives. This is why people who are successful have a consistent schedule. They know that one must repeat the same good habits over a period of time to get results.

According to Rameet Chawla, founder of Fueled, having a consistent schedule aids prioritization, and allows you to keep the important tasks at the top of your list. This is because you are more likely to work harder, and pay more attention when you are in a new, slightly uncomfortable situation. Give some research to determine where you will feel happiest in your new life.

13. ENJOY THE PRESENT MOMENT

I see images of immigrant families and youth who fled their homes for a better life, just like me. I feel blessed in all aspects about my life. I feel like I received a special award when I gained my USA citizenship. For me, it was a historic moment. Through elegant prose, and magic realism, this radical, passionate, real dream which I held in my heart had come true right before my eyes.

If you are constantly dwelling on the past or daydreaming about the future, then you are missing out on the present moment. Remember, everything is possible, but nothing will happen if you do not take action in the present moment. Do your best to become the best winner in this world by being active today toward your dreams. The past and the future are simply illusions. Real life only takes place here and now.

It may seem impossible for some of you to have the life you dream of, yet it's not because you don't have dreams. You lack the willingness to expand your vision. Start paying attention to negative thoughts flowing in your mind so that you can learn to silence them and enjoy the present moment. If a negative thought arises in your head, then acknowledge it, label it a negative thought, and then let it fade away.

STARTING A NEW LIFE FULL OF ENCOURAGEMENT

Keep it simple. You have out of this world talent if you just get out of your own way. Get into the habit of paying attention to the small details around you. Those details will tell you everything you need to know to solve current challenges at hand. Enjoy the process of working through the good and bad occurrences at the present moment. Each will bring back immeasurable feedback, that if paid attention to, signal how to adjust your course of action to live the life you deserve.

If you are conscious enough, you will hear that other people are experiencing life issues too. You will view your own enigmas as nothing in comparison to theirs, thus realizing how blessed you truly are. Appreciate the support of your friends, because they are fans for your success.

Observe small things too like the sun on your skin, or the sensation of your feet walking on the ground, or the artwork in the restaurant you are eating in. Noticing things like these will help you silence a rambling mind and appreciate every moment.

Personally, I love nature. I have always believed that it is time to relax, catch up with family, and enjoy everything; the beautiful fall, or winter weather that brings with it a sense of comfort. I'm especially looking forward this year to spending more time with my children.

We hope we can arrange some sort of getaway trip. Sometimes, the mere thought of doing something adventurous is more appealing than the reality of what we end of doing. As long as we really enjoy the quality moments with each other, the activities are less important.

14. LEARN TO ACCEPT COMPLIMENTS

Become good at receiving compliments with an open heart while building your self-esteem, self-image and confidence. A compliment is a gift to the receiver and a gift to the giver if the receiver really accepts it. The inability to accept compliments is like a plague, helping to create a society of depressed people with poor self-images.

"God blesses those who patiently endure testing and temptation, because after overcoming them, will receive the crown of life that God has promised to those who love him."

-James 1:12 NTV.11.

Very few people accept compliments well. If you don't accept the gift of a compliment, it hurts the giver's feelings and decreases the chance of that person giving you this gift again. Know that some have it better than you, but many have it worse.

When we make ourselves miserable by comparing ourselves with others, we are wasting time and energy that we could use in building our own inner resources. Compliment yourself every morning as you start your day. Being happy makes you a more positive person, which helps you put those positive vibes out into the world.

STARTING A NEW LIFE FULL OF ENCOURAGEMENT

You have your own unique gifts and talents. Focus on sharing them with the world instead of focusing on the gifts of another. Be comfortable with who you are and feel connected to your life in a way you've never done before. Always follow the direction from GOD as he will lead you straight to the top.

15. BECOME AWARE OF RECENTLY EXPERIENCED MAJOR LIFE EVENTS

I'm sure you have had great major life events such getting married, a death in the family, a loss of a relationship, etcetera. This is not uncommon, considering at this moment so many divorces occurring in this world. There are so many children without a family and mothers without support or job. A change in your financial or health status, moving to a new place, or becoming pregnant, can all have a profound effect on your emotions.

"Darkness cannot drive out darkness, only light can do that. Hate cannot drive out hate, only love can do that."

-Dr. Martin Luther King Jr

A negative isn't always a negative. We will lose time focusing on the "why me" hurtful self-blame talk. Many of these thoughts can now start to fade to the background as our greater purpose comes into view. We endure situations which become a testimony to encourage others that life gets better. Some of these may make you happier, while others can trigger stress, depression and or anxiety.

Essentially, some people get knocked down in order to build back up physically, mentally and spiritually. Their strength become our own as well. Sometimes you just have to go through some bad things to appreciate all that GOD has blessed you with and to understand what's really important to you.

Realize that GOD gives us a new opportunity to start a new life, instead of just losing our life completely when we are faced with tragedies and life threating situations. If you have just experienced a major life event, keep in mind that your personal judgment may not be functioning at its best, and consider waiting to make any major life decisions.

If you have just experienced a major loss, allow yourself time to grieve. Mourning is a necessary process of examining and processing your feelings of grief and adjusting to life after your loss. You don't have to feel rushed into changes or pressured to "get over it" right away.

Many of us would have collapsed and given up on life in a situation like this, instead of only reacting and being angry. I encouraged myself to get strong, to restore my strength that I have in me. After so many years there is not room for negative talk and I believe everything happens for a reason because something miraculously and supernatural protects my life every day. It is the love of GOD which continues to change my life for the better.

For example, when we love others, we speak up for what is right. Many hopes, dreams and partnerships die because of words unspoken. Love confronts weeds in the garden. Love encourages, love repeats and love gives life. If you care enough, then open your mouth. If you do care, speak up. What is meant to be will resonate and become. You must respect your voice. Your future, your vision and your destiny is in your mouth. Give it life, speak from the heart, watch it manifest.

16. CHOOSE SUCCESS AS YOUR DESTINED RESULT

The moment you begin anything, make a choice to be victorious. It will cause every nerve and fiber in your being to instantly align itself toward your upcoming success. Everything is a determination of your free will choices. Encourage yourself to make these changes much sooner rather than later. When your determination changes, everything will begin to move in the direction you desire.

Big-scale life do-overs require the same amount of belief in yourself, just the same as very small life changes. Starting a new life is a choice away and you have to be the one to make the choice. You must know you will be successful no matter how much change your life needs. In general, you'll probably need to focus on changes in various aspects of your life including:

1) career

2) emotional

3) physical

4) geographical

5) social

6) financial.

If you have negative thinking such as, "This is never going to work out," then at that very moment, every cell in your body will accept defeat and give up the chance to win. Motivation comes from being excited about the changes, and viewing the changes as an adventure and a unique opportunity to improve your life and the lives of others.

Also, it is best to make these changes before you feel totally ready. Your ego wants you to procrastinate forever, but your higher self is smarter, since it knows that you are ready right now. There really is no better time than the present to begin. Now is your time to begin the road to success.

"A pessimist sees the difficult in every opportunity, an optimistic sees the opportunity in every difficulty"

-Winston Churchill

Do you know why some people do not appear to support or believe in you and in your dreams. Those people are insecure about themselves, and they want to project their insecurities on you so you will start to think and become just as unsuccessful as them.

A successful person inspires, motivates, builds you up. They push you to become better. An unsuccessful person will only blame, hate and complain about everything they observe regarding you. I believe the magic lays inside of a determined mind, a strong will and endless possibilities.

Don't listen to the negative, unsuccessful naysayers. Be determined, filled with a firm purpose; yes, a wholesome worthwhile resolve which will silence your inflated or deflated ego. Being firm in your purpose will ensure you stay on track and do not slip more away from the success you seek.

17. EXAMINE YOUR PAST

There's nothing more special than the love and support of Family. It feeds our souls. I discovered that being a strong women inspired me to do better and become better because GOD give me another opportunity in my life.

Make sure that starting a new life is as effective as you hope. Be certain you're making this change for the right reasons, not as a way to run from your past. Running away from your problems doesn't fix them.

Do you have a habit of trying to "move past" or escape adversity as soon as it comes up? Research suggests that the necessary process of growth comes from working through both positive and negative emotions. How do you react when the going gets tough?

Do you stick to your goals, or do you just get scared and run away? There's nothing better than being the new you. The amazing feeling inside to become more. Every new day is a once in a lifetime opportunity. Don't miss today worried about tomorrow.

The only person you are destined to become is the person you decide to be.

-Ralph Waldo Emerson

18. TAKE YOUR DREAMS OFF THE SHELF AND LIVE THEM

I help many people who have been victims of domestic violence. My ultimate dream, however is to build a big temple for GOD. Why not? I definitely have the talent and strength to go after my dreams.

Unfortunately, having the financial resources to make this dream real is equally important. But I know GOD will provide the avenue and direct me to his amazing plan to achieve this. I may not fathom this plan now, but it will happen. Amen!

People need to realize; our dreams can come true. If each one of us constantly thinks about our only our challenges, then we will not be resolved to reach lofty dreams. This world will be completely different if people would just compromise to take action with stern determination.

All of us have tremendous qualities, yet we need to get out of our own way. This is why it's so important to forgive your past, because you can't motivate yourself with your future plans otherwise. Wrong thinking keeps people stuck right where they are.

If you think you'll never accomplish your dreams, those thoughts will hold you back. Don't limit yourself with defeating thoughts. You should instead fill your mind with very encouraging messages! Please ask God to give you the wisdom to make the right decisions, at the right time, for the best purpose. Ask for GOD to direct you to your amazing future plan.

As a business woman, I have many titles. It's important for me to balance the demands of each role. Experiences help us to reach the new level because plans can change in one's life. It works the same whether it's a big meeting, such as our event with hundreds in attendance, or just a 1 on 1 meeting with someone needing my help. Either way, everyone expects performance in some way; meaning they will get uplifted by me.

I acknowledge that working in business can be a difficult challenge. Sometimes, it is just not simple, but you need to develop your best skills. No matter how much competition you face, you need to confidently give the best of you and show the world who you are.

You need to engage with creativity and passion. You can control your life. You can make this choice. Start immediately and do it flamboyantly; no exceptions. You intuitively already know what changes you need to make. What is stopping you is that you're not quite ready to make these changes yet.

For example: After 2 fabulous years working with a lot people, I'm about to take off on a new adventure. I'm very happy to announce that I will be joining the best life inspiration authors with my own first book. Yes, this book that you are immersed in enjoying right now.

This is an exciting move for my career. Being an Author of a book has been one of my bigger dreams for so many years. What I share in the pages of this book are a special gift that I've held in my heart. This magic can transpire because of all the wonderful people I have met.

I'm blessed to have excellent friends. Thank you for making my dream come true. All of you are so special. GOD pushes me to the next level to start things that I never did before, such as taking this dream off my shelf, so I could live it.

"My only thing is, I'm like. What's next? Because I didn't dream big enough for what I could do."

-Mindy Kaling

So what about you? What do you want to do with your life? What are your dreams? If you could write your best life story today, what would it say? Is your first reaction to hesitate?

Perhaps, you most often see and describe yourself in terms of past experience or present limitations. Perhaps you see yourself more in terms of losing or just surviving rather than fulfilling your dreams. If you packed away your dreams, dare to unpack them today. It's time to enlarge your vision by enlarging the boundary of your territory.

The Unlimited God truly means to grow huge, to grow wide, to go way beyond, to make more room, to increase your capacity, to break out, to breakthrough, to expand, to go further, to occupy new territories, to reserve no limit's, to keep no boundaries, to think big, to be broadened, and to live robust. Enlarging your personal territory is not a mere suggestion, rather it is a life command to develop greater performance in your life.

19. BE THE PERSON YOU WANT TO BE

My life improved because of my ambitions. Many people call me the BIG BOSS WOMAN. I agree it's an honor to hear that, but I do what I do not for some fancy trophy or acknowledged title. Definitely, the biggest moment in my career is when I help any women who is a victim of domestic violence. I can't believe I help so many people, every day, in so many ways.

I love what I do. I openly have Love for all of you that have loved me through the tough stuff. When sad times happened, I said, "Love is all we have and all we take with us". I feel I'm intelligent, interesting, and an attractive woman. I have had moments of doubt, yet my own voice of convictions made the difference. "But I'm so smart and beautiful and powerful" are the words I would often utter softly out loud to encourage myself to be the person I want to be.

It's not about being an imperceptible woman. It's about what you need to do on the way of feeling great and just being amazing, especially when you don't feel all that great about YOU. It's the low self-esteem underlying these complaints; that's the barrier to your true life. Denigration is a problem in relationships. It keeps the focus on another person instead of yourself. Self-denigration is equally a poor choice as you wither away your own self-respect in the process.

STARTING A NEW LIFE FULL OF ENCOURAGEMENT

It is a burden when you don't have the appropriate support systems in place. You must repeatedly, more than one time every day, affirm your destiny. Some people talk about superficial issues and accomplish very little. This prevents more constructive, deeper discussions. Being judgmental creates negativity, especially if it is self-directed.

Dwelling on one's own flaws indicates a critical tendency that can just as easily be directed to one's partner. These same issues apply to friendships too. Yet, it's hard to dissuade women from dwelling on their flaws because low self-esteem is usually deeply rooted in early life experiences. The remnants of these painful experiences may dreadfully be carried forward into current and future self-sabotaging thoughts and behavior patterns.

The reality is, neither friends nor partners should look for perfection, and if they do, it's a red flag for far bigger problems. What does appeal is confidence, authenticity, empathy, and a fun-attitude. As we all know, first we have to love ourselves. Love for others is an extension of this self-love.

It's all the unique talents that you have that help you become the person you dream to be. Change your life by focusing on motivation. This is an extraordinary piece of the puzzle for creating a happy life. You are a remarkable human. If you would only have the appropriate respect for yourself, then you can develop all the biggest potential that is inside of you ready to be seen.

For example, say that you wanted to be the nicest person ever, then all you would need to do is help people when they needed help.

No need for excuses or taking time to determine if you receive a direct benefit by helping a person. Come from your heart and truly choose to aid another human being. Do unto others as you would have done to you.

Remember that you don't have to wait till some distant time in the future to be the right person. Make up your mind and then act right now. Be the person you want to be beginning today. Don't let imperfections or lack get in your way. Decide you will do this and then just do it.

20. DON'T COMPARE YOUR LIFE TO THE LIFE OF OTHER PEOPLES

One of the best things you can do in life is not compare yourself with other peoples' life. This is because your life rewards you for your own life. You are responsible for your new life and happiness. You need to recognize your own behavior, and what is the best solutions for your life.

Prepare yourself mentally to not accept any type of rejection or upset others may spew at you. Stay strong and remember that you aren't dealing with a level headed person at that moment; they are full of toxicity. Right minded people do not act in this manner.

Toxic, negative energy is also a form of denial which those people are exhibiting. Women, you must know that you are as powerful as you want to be. Unite with positivity and self-belief instead of sadness and self-doubt.

Unfortunately, many people measure their own success by comparing it to the success of those around them. It's very real that some people are more obsessively concerned about the lives of other people. If you want to feel accomplished and happy, you will have to stop comparing your life to other peoples' lives.

Many people have the tendency to compare the low points of their own lives with the high points of other peoples' lives. Remember, no matter how perfect somebody's life may seem, behind closed doors, everybody deals with tragedy, insecurity, and other difficulties. These are of the some of the greatest role models that help teach you; follow their lessons and you will never ever go in the incorrect direction.

21. CHOOSE TO SEE MISTAKES AND REJECTIONS AS OPPORTUNITIES TO LEARN

The real magic happens once you have integrity. Once you stand for something and once you assert your needs- which doesn't and shouldn't mean just being an amazing woman. Learn from your past, but don't stay stuck in it. Share your plans with those who love and support you. You'll want that support to help you start fresh life.

Make sure to have a plan. Get yourself organized before attempting to start a new life. You may make mistakes, but never repeat the same mistakes. Learn from your mistakes and help yourself grow stronger as a person. Remember, happiness is a state of mind.

The only thing in the world that we can control is ourselves, so choose to be happy and control yourself by purposely maintaining a positive mental attitude. Learning to adapt to roadblocks and challenges will be necessary as you live your new life.

Starting a new career doesn't mean you'll never feel unappreciated or uninspired again. Moving to a new city doesn't mean you'll never miss home. When you encounter challenges, recognize them as such and do what you need to adapt. You may encounter roadblocks on your journey to your new life. This is normal.

For example, perhaps you wanted to join the Green Berets to fulfill your core values of service and honor, but then you found out that you're too old to enlist. You could view this as a failure and the destruction of your dreams, or you could go back to the drawing board and determine whether there are other things you can do that will also allow you to express those core values.

22. GAIN PERSPECTIVE FROM OTHER PEOPLE

U se 'Aikido' where possible when faced with conflict: reflect the venom from others' attacks away from you, yet be wise enough to turn it into something positive by trying to understand why people are angry. React with gentleness and respect. Practicing gentleness will help you rediscover your sense of wonder as you focus on the positive aspects of life.

This is another great way of appreciating others more and become humbler. The next time you engage in a conversation, let the other person talk. Don't interrupt, and ask questions that make it look like an interrogation. Allow the person to naturally keep talking and sharing.

Though you should contribute to the conversation, make a habit of letting others express themselves more than you do so you don't act like you're only concerned with the things that are going on in your life. Ask questions to show that you understand what the person is talking about.

Don't just wait for the person to stop talking so that you can start talking. Remember, if you're busy thinking about what you want to say, then you'll have a harder time focusing on what they are saying. In contrast, those who can find gratitude in their current existence will be less influenced by those empty promises.

How can we find gratitude in a world that seeks to destroy it? It goes without saying, don't boast about the volunteering you've done. It's great if you're proud of your work, but remember: volunteering is not about you, it is about the people you have helped. Intentionally choose it. Gratitude will never be a result of your next purchase, success, or accomplishment.

It is available in your heart right now. And you will never find gratitude in life until you intentionally decide to choose it. Open your eyes to those with less. Almost half the world, over 3 billion people, live on less than $2.50 per day. 1.1 billion people have inadequate access to clean water, and 2.6 billion lack basic sanitation.

Let those facts sink in for just moment and slowly allow gratitude and a desire to become part of the solution to take their place. Admit that you're not the best at everything or anything. No matter how talented you are, there is almost always somebody who can do something better than you. Look to those who are better and consider the potential for improvement. Nobody is the best at everything.

Even if you are 'the best' in the world at doing one thing, there are always other things that you cannot do, and may never be able to do. Recognizing your limitations does not mean abandoning your dreams, and it does not mean giving up on learning new things or improving your existing abilities.

Worst case scenario; you spend a day making the world a better place. Best case scenario: you discover your purpose. Win-Win. Being a good person means more than just doing things for others. You have to accept and love yourself before you can put positive energy into the universe.

SECTION IV
<u>ACTION STEPS</u>

1. LET GO OF JEALOUSY AND ANGER TO MOVE FORWARD

Be supportive and encouraging to yourself and others. Jealousy is hard to overcome, but it can be done. Try to realize that you don't have to have the same things as everyone else. Try to stop feeling jealous of other people. When you argue with someone, try to control your anger. Don't hide or be rude when you are in an argument with a friend. Talk to them and work it out.

It is best not to fight fire with fire. Both of you need to take some time to think things over. Say things like, "I want to resolve this with you, because you are such a good friend. Let's take time and think this out." Don't put the blame on others either. Accept what is your fault, thereby talking to others about what they have done to upset you. Always remember that blaming others fosters resentment and negativity.

If you can't let go of your anger, try writing down your feelings. Other tools to help include meditating and managing your thoughts. Don't try to correct people when they're angry by saying something irrational. Just listen with compassion and remain quiet. Say to them, "I'm sorry you feel this way, is there anything I can do to help?" Saying nice things to people is an easy way to spread positivity.

Compliment a co-worker's new haircut or a stranger's dog. Compliment friends who you might normally be jealous of. Giving credit where credit is due. Be respectful as you would want the same respect given to you for an achievement you've accomplished. People rarely take the time to listen to people. Everyone wants to feel important and know that they matter. Take the time to listen to people. Truly pay attention and take time to follow what the person is saying.

Don't get distracted by what's going on around you or play on your cell phone. Be engaged with the person and the conversation. Ask follow up questions on the topic; this helps them know that you're paying attention to them. Be kind and generous to others, liking them for who they are. Celebrate others when good things happen and don't be jealous.

2. FIGURE OUT WHAT EXACT CHANGES YOU NEED TO MAKE

There is an important step that happens prior to reaching success. First, you must define what success means to you. It may take many years to become aware what you want to do with your life. Therefore, you must get clear on your values, interests, and passions. This will assist you on setting goals and provide your life with a strong sense of meaning.

Asking yourself the right questions will lead you to your path with less effort and double guessing yourself.

1) What legacy do you want to leave behind?

2) How would you like others to remember you?

3) How can you improve your community?

4) What subjects interest you the most?

Reach your potential as a human being. You are a person with great potential, just like Michael Jordan, William Shakespeare and many other famous people. Einstein was a human, as was Galileo. Once you realize that you are just as human and equally as capable as anyone else, your journey to unlocking your inner creative mind has begun.

God wants to impart his character and power through us. Please remember, you have something beautiful to offer which is unique and dazzling. This is something only you can create. You may have to color outside the lines once in a while before your masterpiece is complete. Think outside the box as much as you need. It's never too late to begin a new life.

"If we step back and look at the bigger picture of what love is what God created it to be it changes everything"

-1 Corinthians 13:13

The thing I'm realizing about life is that it does not matter where you are or what season you're currently walking through; you'll find yourself in spaces that require you to lead. This comes hand-in-hand with challenges to love. It will just make it harder to escape and really, that's what you're trying to do.

3. PUT ACTION INTO DEVELOPING YOUR NEW LIFE

Look at your schedule this week. Write down 4 things you will do to start discovering your purpose. Write it down just like a doctor's appointment. Write in the day and time you will do it in.

Don't know what to do? Commit 60 Minutes to "Life Reflection" A while ago, someone said that "experience is the greatest teacher". I kindly disagree, experience isn't the greatest teacher. "Experience reflected on is the greatest teacher". Set 60 minutes aside this week to think about your life. Grab a pen and paper and just write.

Ask yourself 2 big questions:

1) What makes you happy in your life?

2) What impact do you want to have on this world?

Write something. You will be amazed at the insights that come out of this. Imagine the impossible. Then take the 1st Step for just one moment. Imagine that you could do anything in the world you want to do.

So, if that were possible, what would you do? If you were going to do that one thing, what is the 1st step that you would need to take to make it happen now; take that first step. What do you want to do with your life? Don't be afraid to stand tall in your truth. Face everything confidently. Fight for your inner peace. Fight for your happiness. Fight for everything and everybody that's important to you!

You are too important to waste your life away! Learn to appreciate and value your life, but most importantly, learn to appreciate and value yourself! You count too, no matter what you've done!

4. MAKE 5 SMALL GESTURES A DAILY HABIT

Successful people have one major secret of success; the following of smart daily habits. I'm very happy in my life, I enjoy challenges, because I learned to embrace the difficulty of them. It's what's helped me grow past my own shortcomings. My attitude is, "it's not a big deal. If we need to do it again, then we have to do it again". With those type of habits, you will acquire all the confidence to know you can do it.

Also, GOD will be the elevator to the next level of victories, because you have such incredible opportunities in your life. Start doing simple things, such as smiling at someone or holding the door open for a stranger. This will help you become a better person. During your day, if you want to conserve your positive energy, do something nice for someone.

It's like a test. If you act unselfishly, the positive energy will be returned back to you in a different way. Don't miss the opportunity to give a nice comment. I remember one day when someone came out of the blue and gave me a surprise; I got some very pretty flowers. Soon enough, these small acts of kindness will become a habit that you don't even have to think about. Daily Habits can change lives and may create new life phases, whatever these may be.

By applying the following 5 Small Gestures on a daily basis, you will release big personal advances:

1) Mindset. When you first get out of bed in the morning, you need to set your mind in the right direction. Declare, "This is going to be a great day." The most important thing is to remember that we are in this world for a definitive propose, and having the proper state of mind as we go through each day sets the tone towards achieving respectable results.

2) Be Specific. So what type of people do you like to be around? That will be your guide for the type of people you want to spend your time with. If you like easy-going, care free individuals, then you don't want to be hanging around two quick-paced attorneys who work 75 hours a week. So be clear about whom you want to align with.

3) Follow Up. In your life, as in all sales oriented businesses, the follow up is everything. Yes, I mean *everything*. Call people back after you meet them. Send them information to look at to further your relationship with them. Check in with them, time after time, after your initially meet them, to follow up and see how they are doing with the information you provided them.

4) Trust. Trust the Universe will send you the right people to associate with. Then do your best, and know that the Universe will send the right people your way. Everyone wins when we just stay in the flow of the Universe. Enjoy the process.

5) Listen. People want to know that you are listening to them. Listen to their needs and individual requirements. Escaping the terrible life one may have requires listening to those who have walked the path you seek to walk and follow their good advice. You can do this. Keep going. Become determined to succeed.

Remember, people want to be around people they like. Truly listening to others is a big component of gaining people's trust of you. If they trust you, then they also will like you.

I know there are a lot of details to focus on. Don't get overwhelmed by these. People want to spend time around someone who enjoys their life and uplifts the people around them. Keeping good quality daily habits just makes it much easier to reduce the stress of going through the process along our journey.

5. SET YOUR GOALS

Your journey must begin with new steps you will take along your road towards your new life. Focus on SETTING distinctly clear personal goals. This will help guide you as you embark on starting your new life. Consider where you see yourself in six months, One year, Three years, Five years, Ten years, and Twenty+ years.

How do you start setting your goals? Start by defining your big goal first, and then break it up into smaller objectives. Then break those down even further into tasks.

Give yourself **SMART** career goals. This means the goals are **S**pecific, **M**easurable, **A**chievable, **R**ealistic, and **T**imely. Decide where you want to be six months from now, one year from now, five years from now. Determine the exact rules of how you will know when you have found success.

For example, follow your gut instincts. Be patient and work hard. You will be recognized for your own talents. If you've decided that you want to start a new career as a police officer to make justice happen, then that's going to be your overall goal.

To accomplish this, you will need to achieve several objectives through the actions you choose to take. Examples of objectives to reach this could be: working on your physical fitness so you can pass the physical test; talking with a police recruiter; and applying to a police academy.

Break those down additionally into specific tasks, like exercising three days a week, looking online for your recruiter's information, and finding out the steps to apply to academies. Make sure that you are as concrete and specific as possible when setting your goals.

"The journey of a thousand miles begins with a single step"
-Lao Tzu

This information can really help you as you pursue setting objectives and accomplishing goals. Some may consider this as a slow start, yet this is a major part of setting up the core of your foundation.

Once you get going, your defining moments can be used to help others with major problems they have too. It's important to be humble and persistent. Always prepare for more and stand strong in what you believe.

For example, always say to yourself, "I'm going to keep sharpening my skills. I know that my life will come to an end SOMEDAY, but I'm going to be a humanitarian example around the world and I'm going to do what I need to do to take as far as I can."

6. REVIEW YOUR GOALS EVERY DAY

As I mentioned in the beginning of this book, I started with my mission to become a better person in my new life. Many suggestions of things that have worked for me I have provided in this very book for your benefit.

My favorite song is "My Way" by Frank Sinatra. That song is the biggest inspiration for me to make new goals. That also reminds me of the lessons and love I received from my grandma. Grandma encouraged me to believe that everything is possible in this world.

The most important thing is that she believed in me. She put me first on everything. She training me to be a child with my own mindset. I so appreciate that. She really opened my eyes when was a child.

How well our mind works will dictate

1) how much joy we experience

2) how successful we feel

3) how well we interact with other people.

By the grace of God, each moment is a new beginning; a new dawn for potential. Our thoughts can become totally different, and as a result our life can be transformed.

God wants us to be completely alive, full of passion, and bursting with joy. King David illustrated God's desire when he wrote, *"You turned my wailing into dancing; you removed my sackcloth and clothed me with joy"* (Psalm 30:11, NIV).

God desires us to experience great joy, and he created us with the capacity to create new goals despite our past and regardless of our current circumstances. Our future can exceed our greatest expectations when we think like God thinks.

"Your attitude, not your aptitude, determines your altitude."

-Zig Ziglar

You may be wondering, "How could I possibly do that. You feel like you've made mistakes in life, and you want to undo them. Perhaps you just don't like how your life is going so you want to pretend it never happened. You can start fresh with a new outlook on life, and watch your old worries disappear.

I have been through very hard times and I have sacrificed for my career and my family but this allowed me to be a stronger. It pushed me to become a better person. Most importantly, you must have the courage to follow your heart and intuition. They (heart and intuition) somehow already knows what you truly want to become. Everything else is secondary.

7. EXERCISE YOUR BODY

Beginning a new chapter of your life may include giving more attention to your body as well. Your body is a very complicated object. Without muscle pulling in every direction, gravity holds you down. Without a strong core to stabilize your trunk, or center to keep you stable, you would be limited in your ability to generate force. Your core must be trained, and trained in all directions.

Posture, arms and leg position, the way you lean, and even joint angles all impact the effectiveness of particular exercises. These exercises can help you figure out what goals to set and what changes you will need to make. Research suggests that doing it can make you feel happier and more motivated.

Talk to your trainer or coach to fine-tune every element of your technique before advancing to higher levels and other exercises. For example, videos may be helpful to emulate the right techniques. Practice your exercise at home and make sure the information provided is reliable. Also practice vision exercises where you take a moment to imagine yourself at some point in the future with the body you want to create.

Incorporate as much detail as you can to create a clear image. For example, you could imagine that you are a successful independent athlete, like a tennis player. Possibly you see yourself as a musician

114

with her own band, who travels around the country giving shows at small venues. Now think about the strengths, skills and power you command in this role. Like lovebirds, this vision and the reality you want to manifest go hand-in-hand.

Take care of your body, it's the only place you have to live.

-Jim Rohn

Similarly, so do the idea of Strength and Power form a strong synergy. Power is essential for speed, and strength is essential for power. You will need to develop the strength. Strength is the force you exert and is developed through progressive resistance training. Make sure you execute good form, maintain good range of motion and take short breaks. You must breathe efficiently, because you are almost there.

Obviously, you can't become a superhero like Superman; that isn't possible or realistic. However, you could imagine what you could do what would be similar to that like a Superman's commitment to justice that you admire. You could imagine yourself fulfilling that mission in some way, such as becoming an attorney or police officer.

Is it Superman's physique that you want? You could imagine yourself becoming fit, or even becoming a personal trainer to help others with their fitness goals. These goals require constant personal development in order to complete. You must think positive. Know that your performance is stellar because you always give the best of you. It's important to maintain a regular training regimen. Remember it's important to train smarter, not harder, to get the results you want.

8. TRY A NEW POSITIVE THOUGHT STRATEGY

Apologize to everyone you feel deserves an apology for anything you've ever done to them that could have badly hurt them or insulted them. This will make them feel confident that you can change.

It is impossible to literally think like God as he is all-knowing and all powerful, but we can focus our thoughts on the things that reflect and honor his character. To do this, we must become intentional about mirroring his image in all that we think and do.

Although you may fear that people will be angry and frustrated with you, it is always better to admit this, than to cover it up. Whether you've made a mistake as a boss, parent, or friend, people will appreciate the fact that you're willing to admit that you're not perfect, and that you're working to improve yourself and the situation.

Admitting your mistakes shows that you're not stubborn, selfish, or unwilling to look imperfect. Admitting your mistakes will make people respect you more, whether they are your own children or your coworkers. Commit to conquering this fear.

Start with baby steps. What action can you take today that would move you towards eventually destroying this fear. Recognize your own faults. We judge others, because it's a lot easier than looking at ourselves.

Unfortunately, it's also completely unproductive, and in many cases, harmful. Judging others causes strife in relationships, and it prevents new relationships from forming. Perhaps, even worse, it prevents us from trying to improve ourselves.

Everybody makes mistakes. We make judgments about others all the time, usually without even realizing it. As a practical exercise, try to catch yourself in the act of judging another person or group of people, and whenever you do, judge yourself instead.

Consider how you can improve yourself, instead of how you think others should act. After all, you cannot control other people's decisions and behaviors - but you can control yours. Work to address your flaws.

9. READ INSPIRING IDEAS EVERY DAY TO KEEP "WONDER" IN YOUR LIFE

Use some inspirations to help yourself become a better person. Children possess a sense of wonder at the world that is difficult to replicate as an adult. Spend more time around kids and see how they appreciate the world, are constantly questioning it, and how they get pleasure and joy out of the smallest and most mundane things.

To a child, a flower or a toilet paper roll can be the most incredible thing in the world, at least for an afternoon. Spending more time around children will remind you of how magical the world really is. The greatest impediment you face to discovering your purpose is your own self-doubt.

Therefore, it is critical that you defend yourself against these woeful voices of doubt and insecurity. The simple way to do this is to commit to reading 30 to 60 minutes of inspiring books every single day. Imagine feeding your mind every day with some of the greatest and most inspiring thinkers in all of human civilization.

Do you think that will impact your sense of possibility? Yes, it will. As you read more, your sense of possibility will increase. As your sense of possibility increases, you will start to be more comfortable.

10. BEGIN TO MAKE SMALL CHANGES

No one can change immediately, but even small changes can make an enormous and positive difference. Start with a proper nutrition, hydration and sleep. These are all helpful in maximizing your progress.

The trick is knowing how much is right for you. When you are depressed, your body needs more time to fully recover. Could you set small goals every month or two and focus on one or two key habits which you want to change.

For example, two habits may be as follows:

1) I will listen to others without interrupting at all, either verbally or in any other way. Think of how annoying it can be for you when the other person begins to move their lips as if they are about to intervene.

2) I will do my best to think of what things would make another person happy. This could be sharing your food or drink with others when they are hungry or thirsty, letting someone else sit where you want to sit, or something else.

Be for real. Don't allow your goals to be only abstract dreams. Write them down, and then make a list of what you have to do in order to obtain them. Post them on your bedroom wall. Add them to your daily "to-do" list and share them with your family, friends, coaches and teammates.

Before you know it, those "to-do's" will be so etched in your mind they'll begin to show up on your reality. I never run away from my own big goals, yet knew that I would need smaller goals as I progressed to get there.

For example, find a life coach. They have developed mental techniques and mantras that propel them to be at their best no matter what. Then they share these ideas with their clients. I think people that are most informed of strategies that work and apply them will perform well consistently.

11. DO AN ACT OF CHARITY FOR SOMEONE ELSE

Every day, do something nice for someone, even if it's something small. An act of kindness and generosity can have a great influence. Smile, hold the door open for someone, pay it forward at the drive through; just try to do something to make someone's day. This act makes me reflect on how much or how little we have in our lives.

For example: sometimes I think about my classmates. Because we all went to the same school and we lived in a similar neighborhood. However, some of my classmates had advantages in certain areas and now they are professionals, whereas the others are not.

"You should go out each day expecting good things, anticipating God's blessings and favor. God has planned all of your days for good, not evil."

-Joel Osteen

I realize that all of us have the same opportunities, yet we end up in different places. Some of us get advancement in our careers and others get too comfortable in the middle of their dreams and settle for less.

STARTING A NEW LIFE FULL OF ENCOURAGEMENT

I believe our abilities and initiative to seize opportunities ultimately determines how successful we become. Success is not measured by how much money a person amasses. Being a successful person for me is about how many people you can help every day with your aptitude.

Did you help people who have been cold or indifference to you? Show someone who is rude to you the example of your kindness. Maybe, people have always been rude to them. Be the person who shows them kindness instead of ignoring them.

I believe this society is filled with unprecedented pressure. People are getting divorced at higher rates than ever. Some children have to deal with drugs, guns and sex in their neighborhoods and near their schools.

Commercials and movies are heavily promoting alternative lifestyle, promiscuity, greed, violence and pornography. Many people work eight hours a day or more and then come home to prepare meals, do laundry, clean and care for the children. They face an immense financial pressure.

This is why we need more and more kind acts in the world. To show mercy and love is a shining path to brighten someone else's day.

12. CHOOSE YOUR ENVIRONMENT

Don't hang on to painful memories and bad feelings, as that's a sure-fire way to encourage negative thoughts and bad moods. Your past can take control of your present, and rob your future if you let it. If you can, forgive past wrongs and move on. This includes forgiving yourself.

Forgiveness is done for your peace of mind and your happiness, not for the other person. Forgiving someone doesn't mean you condone their behavior; wrong is wrong.

The purpose of forgiveness is to set you free, since holding onto anger is like putting yourself in a prison cell. If you have a hard time forgiving or forgetting, consider talking through your emotions with a good friend or counselor, but try not to dwell on the matter.

It's important to work through things, but you can't let the past determine your future. The environment around us has a huge impact on us on all levels of conscious (both subconscious and unconscious). This includes the place we live in, friends we have, things we read, people we see and the list goes on.

Environment is contagious. Thomas A Edison said he was able to become a successful inventor because he placed himself in the company of people who were much smarter than him and then he was able to learn from them.

STARTING A NEW LIFE FULL OF ENCOURAGEMENT

Most likely your thoughts will be correspondent to the environment you subjected yourself to. Have you noticed that you feel serene and calm when you go to a beautiful lake or some beautiful natural environment? This is the reason why you must seek an environment that fits the New you.

13. CHANGE YOUR ENVIRONMENT

Your physical, geographical and social environments make a very noticeable impact on how we feel about our life.

Your physical environment is the entities which you don't spend much time with.

For example, people at the coffee shop, people you say hello to when passing by, people in the grocery store, new people you meet at bars, etc. This usually doesn't have a long term impact on you. Unless you change it into macro environment yourself, you are the environment in this case.

If you have a reactive brain, then most likely you will have reactive thoughts, unless you change your environment. I say there are many behaviors that increase self-esteem, enhance your self-confidence and support your motivation. Incorporate these habits to become a more confident person today. The entities with which we spend most of our time lie in Macro environment.

The place you live, the place you work, the colleagues, friends with whom you spend most of the time etc. All these are part of environment. It's very important that you put yourself in an environment which motivates you constantly to become successful. It will <u>always</u> take work, dedication, and patience. It can be stressful and intimidating.

126

STARTING A NEW LIFE FULL OF ENCOURAGEMENT

Sometimes, moving to a new place is enough to feel like you're starting a new life. You probably have a new job, and have to build a new circle of friends. Hence, you have to get used to the new community you've entered. You will need to learn to be self-reliant, to build new connections, become more flexible, and adaptable. These are all excellent skills for your new life.

Things to consider where to move include the crime rate, the unemployment rate, the average cost of living, property cost, and whether there are experiences available that match your culture and interests. You can also consider quality of living rankings.

If you can, talk to people who live in places you're considering moving to. Plan a visit to see whether you would enjoy living there. The more information you can gather, the better prepared you will be to embark into your new environment to live your new life.

Starting a new life can be a daunting prospect. Surround yourself with people who love and respect you and can help you on your journey. Knowing that you have sources of emotional support will help you feel strong and capable as you face your new life.

If you don't have family or friends who can support you, consider looking in other places. Support groups and faith communities are common places where people find others to support them.

14. EXAMINE YOUR RELATIONSHIPS

Interpersonal relationships are crucial to improving how you feel about yourself and your life. Research shows that we are highly influenced by the people we interact with, so in starting your new life, choose the people to include who matter most to you. Be wise who you are around and choose the ones who will give you the love and respect you deserve.

It's hard to start a new life if you have toxic people dragging you down. In some cases, you must cut people out of your life for your own safety. In other cases, they're simply not good for you to spend time with, and you'll be happier if you remove them from your life. You will want to be aware of tell-tale red flag signs that a person isn't good for you.

Sometimes you feel exhausted by spending time with them, or you dread interacting with them. They are hyper-critical or judgmental of you. You feel like you can't do anything right when you're around them. They say mean or vicious things about you, to your face or behind your back.

You feel obsessive about this person, as though you can't live without them, even if they don't pay attention to you. You constantly feel stressed out when you're around them. You don't feel safe sharing your hopes, thoughts, needs, or feelings with them.

STARTING A NEW LIFE FULL OF ENCOURAGEMENT

Recovering addicts often must learn to avoid the places where they used to spend time, as well as many of their old friends, in order to avoid addiction triggers that could cause a relapse. If you are a recovering alcoholic, spending time with your old drinking buddies in your favorite bar would probably put far too much pressure on you and could cause you to take up drinking again.

Forming a supportive social network that doesn't involve your past habits is critical to maintaining your successful recovery. It may also be helpful for you to make social changes if you are recovering from domestic or relationship abuse. Many victims of domestic abuse have been isolated by their abusive partners until they have very few connections that are not carefully monitored or controlled by the abuser

Learn to find sources of social support. The caring of others is very helpful in starting a new life after surviving abuse. You could consider finding support at support groups for domestic abuse survivors, in your faith community, or through mental health provider referrals.

15. CREATE HEALTHY RELATIONSHIPS

I f you have toxic relationships, it can often make your life very hard. Moreover, you probably wouldn't have started a relationship with any person you didn't like the qualities of. Hence, it becomes stressful being in a relationship with a person once you find they are more of a liability to you becoming the new you.

So as difficult as it may be in some cases, this is why eliminating unhealthy social relationships will help you move forward to a happier, healthier life. Evaluate whether you need to cut a person off, and act immediately. Sometimes, loved ones say hurtful things we don't need to hear and it's better to be out of that environment. Instead of focusing on their negative words, replace their criticism with encouragement.

Explain your feelings openly and honestly. See if the person will validate your feelings, apologize and change their ways. If they're not willing to work with you to meet your needs or change their attitude, you don't need that person in your life. This doesn't mean that they're completely a bad person. They are just not a right relationship to have around you. Cut them off so you don't lose more time and receive more hurt from this person.

Before cutting a relationship out of your life, also decide whether the person brings positive things in your life that you want and need, even if sometimes the relationship is hard. Conversely, just because a person always makes you feel good doesn't mean s/he's the best relationship for you. It is often easier for you to stay addicted to substances, but that isn't actually what's best for you neither.

Foster your relationships with people who bring you joy. Make a list of the people who make you feel like you can be a better yourself around. You want to have people in your life that bring you happiness and positivity. Make sure to foster your relationships with healthy relationship driven people, so that you don't feel like you have to keep negative relationships around just so you won't be alone.

If you have decided that a relationship with a person is just unhealthy for you, tell that person that you have to end the relationship for your own well-being. It's important to be always be honest.

Also, if you have people in social media that constantly need to remind you about negative things, you need to block them. Constant reminders of negative thoughts will block the progress you seek. Of course, it's a challenge, but it's important for you for your mental health to not have such energy around you, even in the digital world.

16. GET SUPPORT

When your self-esteem is challenged, don't sit around and fall victim to **paralysis by analysis**. The late Malcolm Forbes said, "Vehicles in motion use their generators to charge their own batteries. Unless you happen to be a golf cart, you can't recharge your battery when you're parked in the garage!"

Gratitude opens the door to simplicity. A person who is grateful for the things they own will care for them, enjoy them, and waste less energy seeking more. They will experience fulfillment in the gifts they already possess, rather than looking outside themselves for more.

Be positive as much as possible. Negativity only hurts yourself and others. If you are negative, it has an impact on the way you treat others. Our mentality can influence the achievements of our days. Focus on what's possible. Avoid "can't" thinking or other negative language.

Don't be afraid to seek help in accomplishing things, but remind yourself that you don't need approval from others to recognize your accomplishments. Focus on what you're able to do. Remind yourself of all your capabilities and positive qualities. Let go of the past; you must look to the future to change.

Stop thinking of old failures. They are the past. This is NOW. Remind yourself that this time you're focusing on the core issues that will ensure your success. Be responsible for your feelings. Just as you can't make other people happy, don't expect others to make you feel happy or good about yourself ... and don't blame them if you feel guilty or bad about yourself.

You create your own feelings and make your own decisions. People and events may set the stage for your emotions, but they can't dictate them. What others think about you and say to you can only have as much effect as you allow it to have. What's important is what you tell yourself, and how you react to others. Be kind to yourself.

17. PLAN SOME CAREER CHANGES

Starting a new career is a great way to reinvent yourself. Plenty of people work at jobs they don't love or don't feel inspired by. Getting out of that rut is an excellent way to start a new life. Figure out what your core values are and decide what career path will allow you to express those values.

Take your current skills and aptitudes into account. What do you know? What are you good at? What unconventional skills do you have? For example, perhaps you're a real "people person" who feels inspired by interacting with others, and you don't get to do that in your current job. This could be something that you're good at and also something that's a core personal value for you.

Don't feel limited by what you currently know or what your current life situation is. No matter where you start, you can become what you want to be. For example, if you decide that because you're a people person, you want to become a therapist or teacher, you will likely need further education, yet you can accomplish that. You're never stuck where you are. Seek a professional to aid you with this task if you feel you are not able to come up with it yourself.

18. TALK WITH OTHERS

When you want to start a new life, it can be helpful to talk to people who are living the type of life that you want. This is helpful because it can give you an idea of how to get there. For example, if you want to drop your 9-to-5 corporate drone job and become a life coach in Fiji, it would help if you could find out what other life coaches did to get themselves there so you have a roadmap.

Asking people about their paths also allows you to build support networks that can be very helpful in setting out on your new life. It's also a very good idea to ask people hard questions about your new life. It can be easy to idealize a new career or new community. Understanding the nitty-gritty details of what you're about to embark on will help you stay the course even when you encounter roadblocks.

For example, you might daydream about ditching your boring job in North Dakota and moving to Hawaii, where life is paradise. However, if you talked to people who live there, you might discover things you didn't know, such as the fact that it's incredibly expensive; healthcare is often hard to find. Also, if you aren't island-born with Native Hawaiian or Asian ancestry, you'll always be a haole, or a "foreigner" in the local people's eyes.

That wouldn't mean you wouldn't love your decision to move, but this knowledge would help you adjust to the realities of your new Life better.

.

19. CHOOSE A ROLE MODEL

Great role models give folks good moral values to live by. They teach you the importance of morals. Sometimes, they may feel as if their efforts were in vain, because you may not show signs of change right way.

They must realize that planting the good seed in your mind is what matters and that seed may bloom at some point later on. It may take some time to respond to the good lessons, but at some point you will.

Having a role model provides you an example of someone to correspond to. This person should have trait's you want to attain. Think of ways how you can better embody the qualities you admire. Think of how to apply those qualities in your work, creative pursuit's, personal relationships, diet, and lifestyle.

Who do you look up to and why? How are they making the world a better place to live in, and how can you do the same? What qualities do you admire in them, and how can you develop the same ones?

Keep your role model close to you, like a friendly spirit that is always at your side. Think how they would respond to a question or circumstance, and how you could respond in the same manner. Live your life in a way that inspires others. Share your life and philosophies with others.

As you become more aligned to your new destiny, you will want to pay the same role model support forward to another deserving individual who needs the help, just like you did. Find someone you can be a role model to.

Be cautious of the way you live, so that you will always be acting in a way that will make someone proud. Start small. Join a Big Brother-Big Sister program, volunteer to coach kids' sports team, teach, or be a role model for young family members.

20. EVERY DAY, BECOME A BETTER YOU

Challenge yourself to look at others and appreciate the things they can do, and more generally appreciate people for who they are. Understand that everybody is different, and relish the chance you have to experience different people.

You will still have your personal tastes, your likes and dislikes, but train yourself to separate your opinions from your fears. You will appreciate others more. You will be humbler as well. Being able to appreciate the talents and qualities of other people can also make you recognize qualities that you want to improve or attain within yourself.

While competition can be healthy and stimulating, it's nearly impossible to be humble when we're constantly striving to be the "best" or trying to be better than others. Instead, try looking at yourself more. Remember, the ultimate goal isn't to be better than anyone else, it's to be better than the person you used to be.

When you focus your energy on improving yourself instead of comparing you to everyone else, you'll find that it is much easier to make yourself better since you don't have to worry about whether or not you're better or worse than anyone. Every individual is unique.

Appreciate people for who they are as human beings, not for their skills and appearance in relation to yours. Don't be afraid to defend others judgment. Although it is ultimately up to you to, decide if you were right or wrong. It is a whole different thing to acknowledge that you make mistakes and that you're not always right.

Somewhat more difficult, however, is the ability to acknowledge that in many cases other people even people who disagree with you may be right. Deferring to your spouse's wishes, to a law you don't agree with, or even, sometimes, to your child's opinion takes your recognition of your limitations to a different level.

Instead of simply saying you are humble and as a person you will make mistakes, you should also concentrate on living with that mindset that being humble is a way of life, not just a one-time action.

21. MANAGE YOUR FINANCES

Since I opening my first company, I became very strong in all areas. I see things are coming along with sustained perseverance. Running a business, is not easy but I love management, especially regarding overseeing the financial aspects of the business.

I am continually learning strategies how to manage money and get help to ensure my financial stability increases over time, regardless of income levels. I'm not afraid of challenging myself to become smarter about money all the time.

I have another important concept that has helped me which you can use too; keep track of your personal and business expenses. Review your bank statements often to assure you are not outspending your earnings and savings.

It also ensures that your bank statements are correct. If you spend your money, be in control and accountable for your financial activities. Never play the "I don't know what happened to my money" game.

If you do your banking online, be sure to keep personal records on paper ledgers and/or portable financial money management apps as well. The better you are aware of the flow of your money, the easier life will become for you. Once you understand your income and expenses, you can more efficiently plan out what level of lifestyle it will accommodate.

Talk with your accountant to determine your net income. Be sure to consider how federal, state, and social security tax deductions from your gross pay will affect your net income. It is very important to follow all regulatory laws concerning your earnings, especially if you have any investments.

You may have some write-offs that will offset your expenses, thus reducing your legal tax liabilities. Your financial professional will be your champion to know how all the pieces of your financial puzzle fit together.

Your net pay is the amount of money you end up keeping to use as you see fit. Pay attention and prioritize spending. Your first priority should be spending money on basic necessities like food, shelter, and clothing. Please don't spend money on luxuries like expensive clothes, cars, or vacations until you have first satisfied your basic necessities.

Be honest with yourself and differentiate between your basic needs and your luxuries. Be smart and save money. Every month, you should deposit some of your money into a savings account and let it accumulate. Consider asking your employer to directly deposit a portion of your income into your savings account.

If you dedicate yourself to being financially responsible, you can award yourself at a later time with something that makes you happy; an example would be a delicious dinner in a good restaurant with your family.

STARTING A NEW LIFE FULL OF ENCOURAGEMENT

Whatever the positive self-reward might be, enjoy it without guilt as you deserve to be happy for all the hard work you perform in your life. Celebrate the little victories too, as it provides motivation and reinforcement to keep going on the path you are on.

22. START A NEW FINANCIAL LIFE

Whether you've just graduated from college or have been working for 35 years, it's never too early or too late to start a fresh financial life. Perhaps you want to start saving for a major life goal, such as buying a house or retiring. Perhaps you want to revamp your spending habits so that you don't waste as much money.

Take a look at your goals and decide how you need to manage your money to get you there. You may find consulting with a financial planner helpful, especially if your goals are significant or complex, like starting a small business. Examine your finances. Determine your net worth to give you a snapshot of what you owe and what your assets are.

This will help you make good money decisions. People who have just gotten married will also benefit from taking a good look at their finances. You will likely want to form a budget, add each other as beneficiaries on any retirement and insurance plans, and consider a new insurance policy. If you have more debts than you can possibly manage to pay, you may consider filing for bankruptcy.

Depending on the amount of debt and your income, most of your debts will be wiped out and you can start a new financial life. However, this is a very serious decision that has long-lasting effects on your credit and overall well-being, so you should not make this decision lightly. Speak with a bankruptcy attorney to determine whether this is a suitable option for you.

23. MANAGE YOUR TIME

Time management is one of the most important success skills. It's important to manage your time, so that you have enough time to complete any given task effectively. Use a paper or electronic planner to help keep you organized throughout your days, weeks, and months.

Putting off important tasks until the last minute will cause you undue stress. Think how much you can be achieve within the hours of each day when you limit unnecessary activities that are not the pressing priority.

To accomplish more each day, reduce time stealers such as distractions (people interrupting you away from your priority activity), meetings (unproductive talking about ideas without actual doing) and environmental noises (loud music playing or people talking too excitedly around you).

In the end, of course, the time management process takes consistence implementation to reach your destiny. Success doesn't happen by accident, but because you have committed yourself to certain productive activities, that will help you reach your goals faster.

Make a list of all the things you need to do in a given day, and check off each task as you complete it. This will help you stay organized and motivated.

24. DEVELOP NEW SKILLS AND IMPROVE OLD SKILLS

Being proactive and active could help to improve your skills. I always believe and I have utmost faith that everything is possible in this world. Please remember this! When you find your mission and purpose, only then, can you can strengthen your skills.

I recommend attending trainings because they are an excellent way to help people with developing purpose and to become more confident. This in turn makes one become less dependent on others. They will have acquired the skills how to overcome everyday challenges.

It's an important distinction to make between perspective of practice and work. The goal of practice is to learn how to learn new skills. Be ready for the difficulty of deliberately practicing those creative skills. I suggest that every day you must practice the new routine and find the right perspective.

The goal of work is to accomplish something worthwhile. An example could be getting healthy in your life. As a professional, I know how important it is to trust in yourself. It's not impossible to separate out the components, but you must love yourself more than anything.

For instance: You can be active and focus on practicing a few notes of a piano piece. It's so easy to use a video website like YouTube nowadays and watch video lessons about piano. It is super important to keep improving yourself.

If you choosing one element to develop getting better with, let it be to "work with passion". You want to improve that talent every day. An architect, perhaps would consider possible materials or how to use an area of space.

Yes, there are many variables, yet you will concentrate on improving the quality of your work and learn any skills necessary to get you closer to your desired result. Develop solid techniques and know how to apply them in actual life. If you want to learn self-defense, build confidence or stay in shape. Some people aspire to reach the competitive level with their skills and that is ok too.

"The greatest way to live with honor in this world is to be what we pretend to be."

-Socrates

Be creative. You need to develop your own techniques and know how to apply discipline and commitment to consistent learning. The key in life is about being smart enough to demonstrate to yourself that you did. Sometimes, you need to redo old work. Do the work first, then go back and redo all, especially if you are dissatisfied with the result. It is ok to create something new.

STARTING A NEW LIFE FULL OF ENCOURAGEMENT

Don't worry! Just believe in the angels. They will delivery many skills to stimulate the process. Once you make some progress, you can switch which elements you need to free up and fix things. Keep repeating it until the skills as a whole improves. You must think about things a little different.

I have realized that, in general, complete freedom is putting your talents to work to pursue your dreams. With that, you provide yourself constrained effort to be free. You can create awesome things once those constraints are overcome in new ways.

25. MAKE THE WORLD A BETTER PLACE THROUGH YOUR SHINING EXAMPLE

Did you recognize yourself in someone else's perilous life storms, especially with how they deal with major life challenges? Why not help someone who is going through the same struggles?

Every time you interact with the world, you have an opportunity to do something good and positive. It does not have to be something big, but can be something like picking up some trash that someone else carelessly threw down in a local park or in front of your neighbor's home.

For example: Let's say that your child comes home excited because he won a medal at a school event. But what do you do if the same child comes home empty handed instead? As a parent, all we can do is encourage our children and refuse to let them become disillusioned or depressed.

We can tell them they may not have won today, but there is always tomorrow. Obviously we feel this way about our own natural children, but we can also help the world with this type of loving encouragement too. I certainly feel we can all do it. We must be conscientious and find a way to give back to the world.

Easy ways to make a positive change include:

1) Recycling

2) Buying organic

3) Buy locally grown food

4) Be a responsible pet owner by cleaning up after your pets

5) Donate old items to shelters or charitable organizations instead of just a thrift store.

6) Put items back in the proper location in a store where you got them instead of leaving them in the wrong location

7) Refrain from taking the closest parking space, so you leave it for someone who needs it more

If you are not in the middle of a life challenging storm now, why not help someone who is going through one. I believe in the word of deliverance and breakthrough. Let's be a force to help others actualize this too.

26. DECIDE THE CHANGES YOU WANT TO MAKE

I decided to change my life and I developed a different kind of closeness to GOD. He gave me comfort and peace in my heart. For some people, starting a "new life" might mean beginning everything over: relocating, building new social networks, getting a new job, etc.

For others, it might mean smaller but substantive changes, such as ditching old sabotaging habits or perspectives and focusing on developing new, value driven ways of living that are more congruent to your life. Whatever you desire, make sure you are clear about how big the changes are that you want to make.

Figuring out what about your life needs to change can be very helpful here. For example, what is making you unhappy or dissatisfied? Do you need to change every single thing about your life, or would it be more effective to focus in on one or two areas?

I constantly wanted to tell my friends and my family about how important it is to change our life, little by little. I felt a supernatural peace in my heart from GOD and he renewed my strength to restore my life.

I began to learn how to express myself with GOD and I have a very strong connection. He is close to me during the spiritual rehabilitation period. I always say ***"The Lord is my strength and song, and is become my salvation"*** (KKV).

Making change is hard, but nothing is impossible. Pray for this powerful blessing so you can receive it daily in your life. You can't simply tell yourself to start re-categorizing from now on, or to be open to new information, or to stop taking a single perspective.

So you might find better success if you start small and work your way up. Developing a mindful mindset is similar. There are behaviors and certain practices that can help you, while others will only hold you back. Therefore, you must choose wisely what behaviors you will embrace.

Think about yourself for a moment. You are an amazing human being who is so lovely and caring, with an indomitable spirit, a laugh out-loud sense of humor and incomparable zest for life. You're one of a kind. That wouldn't work by itself to create the new life you seek. Start now! It's better because there is liberty and joy with the power of GOD.

27. LEARN AS YOU GO WHILE CHASING AFTER WORTHY GOALS

B uild a list of your goals, and plan ways to achieve them. Be sure to address both short-term and long-term goals; try to think beyond financial/career goals. Consider which subjects you enjoyed studying in school, and why. This can help give you an idea of what you may be best at or more interested in.

We all live in the same world. Without having any perspective about solutions to reach goals, we end up hurt each other and get very little accomplished. Being a good person includes not being judgmental.

You need to accept everyone, no matter what race, age, sexual orientation, gender identity, or culture they are. Realize that everybody has feelings, every person is valid, and everyone should always be treated with respect.

Elderly people are mistreated a lot, so we must honor them. When you are out and see an old person alone, say hello with an amiable smile and ask them how they are doing. Just acknowledging someone can really make their day. Realize that you will be old someday and may need a helping hand.

Next time you go to a mall, parking lot, or anywhere, look for an old person struggling with something, like carrying bags or loading groceries into their car. Ask, "May I help you with that?" You will be doing a great service for seniors. Sometimes you may get one who will reject your offer; simply respond, "I understand, and I wish you a good day."

Equally as important, be compassionate towards intellectually challenged people. They are people with feelings too. They may not know how much their ignorance through words and actions is causing harm and hurt to others. Give them a big smile and treat them like a person.

If other people are smiling or laughing with your interaction with them, ignore them and keep your attention on the person who is your true friend. Don't be racist, homophobic, or intolerant of other religions. The world is a large place full of diversity. Learn from others and celebrate differences.

28. MAKE SOME EMOTIONAL CHANGES

I'm writing this book to give my point of view to help others like you. I want to demonstrate that life Changes I received are because of GOD. I have a very strong connection with Him.

Look at yourself and think deeply about the following four questions:

1) Am I happy or not?

2) How do I handle my life with so many things to juggle and different emotions at the same time?

3) How can I take care of my life and my family

4) Am I brave enough to even face my own pain?

Remember, it's all part of the process. Time cures your feelings but it's wonderfully rewarding if you put your trust in GOD's hands. He can change your emotional outlook. You just only need to pray, and ask for this with all your heart. He can give you a new perspective on the world and how to live with it. Really! He will make you feel like you've started a new life.

Self-growth is a continual process that you'll spend the rest of your life working on. Keep a gratitude journal. Gratitude is more than an attitude: it's a way of approaching life, determined to acknowledge even the smallest moments of good and beauty. The most grateful people seem to be the most successful too.

STARTING A NEW LIFE FULL OF ENCOURAGEMENT

Research has shown that practicing gratitude makes you feel happier and more satisfied with life; it helps you learn flexibility and adaptability to change; increases your physical health and sleep quality; and can help you overcome trauma.

Take five minutes every day to record something you're grateful for that day. Explore why you're grateful for it and what it brings to your life.

Forgive. Forgiveness releases you from the burden of past injury and pain. You forgive others, not for them, but for yourself. Studies show that forgiveness makes you feel less angry and anxious.

Grieve losses. Allow yourself to feel grief and loss rather than trying to hurry yourself to "get past it." Properly mourning takes time and patience with yourself. Acknowledging your sorrow is key to working through it, and eventually incorporating it into the new life you build after the loss.

Acknowledge your own needs. People are all too often taught to deny themselves proper self-care. Acknowledge that you have needs, and that it is not selfish to meet them. You don't have to say "yes" to every invitation or request. Taking some time out for yourself is not wrong. Caring for yourself will not only help you feel better, it will help you interact more positively with others.

29. LOOK AFTER YOUR HEALTH

A healthy body supports a healthy mind. Eat a balanced diet and ensure that you aren't lacking in any necessary nutrients. Establish the cause of any problems you may experience, such as lack of energy or lack of concentration. Correct this by talking with a doctor, nutritionist or other health professional.

Get plenty of exercise too, but align it with what you love to do, rather than what you feel you have to do but dislike. Quiet your mind and think only about thinking. Become consciously aware of your thought processes. Are you thinking the right things?

Practice meditation to help you concentrate on your desired topic, or just meditate to rest your brain. A rested brain is much like a rested body; it's functions are quick, fresh, and more useful and exciting. Read anything you can find about

1) How to meditate

2) How to do awareness meditation

3) How to meditate with your inner voice.

Use meditation to help increase your motivation to make positive life changes. Our lives can pull us in so many different directions that at times (well, at least most of the time) we can feel like there is just no more to give. You know exactly what I mean.

It's really sad that it almost takes a breakdown for us to realize:

1) How much we need to rest

2) How much we need to slow down our pace

3) How much we need to decompress

4) How much we need to just sit still.

It's not an act of laziness or selfishness if you decide to take a break. It is actually a sign of self-control and self-respect.

We all need to think of ourselves as much as we think of others, because if we are weak and worn down, we cannot be strong when others need us. In the next few days, do something just for you. If you can't take a whole day, then take 1 hour, just for you.

Think of something you love to do that makes you smile and go do that! It's time to show the world around you that you understand your own importance.

Today, I make the time for self-care, no matter what. Take a nap, go for a hike, do yoga, get a massage, drink fresh organic juice, soak in a sea salt bath, or whatever defines self-care for you.

What's your favorite way to take good care of yourself? What will you do today for Self-Care? If you're resisting self-care, or think you're too busy with responsibilities, self-care is part of your responsibilities. It insures you'll live a healthier, happier life. Love your life and yourself! This is a new beginning. Please believe in you

.

30. PLAN TO ACHIEVE PHYSICAL CHANGES

Go for it and make up your mind you will have your desired physical achievements. Allow yourself to have high spirit as you move into action towards your health goals. Most importantly, do not lose your confidence about your health condition. Putting a priority on fitness during the day can make you feel better about creating a fresh life start.

Objectify who is your best looking role model. Once identified, start your pursuit to emulate that person. Change the concepts of how you think about your body and the style you wear. Do not be afraid to show your style, and dress up as if you were in a celebrity red carpet event.

Maybe you've been overweight and this has held you back while hurting you emotionally If your weight is something you'd like to change about yourself, it is best to talk with a doctor about how to lose weight effectively and safely. To feel healthier again, they will probably recommend a combination of exercise and healthy eating habits.

If your weight problems are very serious, the doctor may even recommend medication or some form of a weight-loss surgery. You should always consult with your doctor prior to starting a weight-loss plan. Eating better is simple once you are educated on how to begin.

Take your first step by taking action, even if you are unsure how everything needs to flow. You will get more aware as time goes on. You do not need all the answers on day one to get going towards a better body and wardrobe. I promise that in due time, your chosen clothes will feel better on you as both your self-image and weight get aligned with one another.

Also, please give yourself self-talk that includes positive words as this helps with the process. Rather than thinking of modifying your own eating habits as "going on a diet," think of them as starting a new life-long commitment to healthy eating. Incorporate plenty of fresh fruits, vegetables, lean proteins, and whole grains. Definitely skip on processed and junk foods.

Staying fit is the fifth most popular New Year's Resolution. Unfortunately, about eighty percent of American adults don't get enough aerobic and muscle building exercise. Aim for a minimum of 150 minutes each week of moderate aerobic exercise, and do muscle-strengthening exercises at least two times each week.

Dress to express yourself. How you dress affects how you feel about yourself and consequently how others will perceive you. Studies have shown that when you dress in a way that aligns with your goals, you're more likely to achieve them.

So go ahead, wear that little black dress you've always wanted, or express your favorite fandom with some super rad t-shirts. I do this and I know it works from my own experience.

31. RESPOND TO DIFFICULT MOMENTS BY INCREASING PRODUCTIVITY LEVELS

Lose the guilt. You're not to blame every time something goes wrong or someone has a problem. Apologizing for things and accepting the blame can be a positive quality — if you're in the wrong. You learn and move on. But you shouldn't feel responsible for all problems or assume you're to blame whenever someone's upset.

Many of us know people who seem to start almost every sentence with the words, "I'm sorry." I challenge you to remove the word "sorry" completely from your vocabulary. Every time you say, "I'm sorry," you reinforce his idea that you're less than you should be in your subconscious mind. If you're wrong, use the words "I apologize" instead and stop telling yourself and everyone around you that you're sorry.

Even if you don't think anything is "wrong," it could be helpful to see a counselor or therapist when you're considering starting a new life. You'll be making some major life changes, and stress pretty much always accompanies decisions like this. A therapist will give you a safe "sounding board" to explore your hopes and fears as you make these changes. They can also help you learn helpful ways of thinking and reacting to challenges.

STARTING A NEW LIFE FULL OF ENCOURAGEMENT

Many people believe that people with only "everyday" issues wouldn't benefit from therapy, or that it's only for people with "serious" problems. The truth is, going to a therapist can be a lot like seeing your dentist for a cleaning: you're dealing with little buildups of minor problems before they become disastrous.

Some people believe that seeing a therapist is a sign of weakness or that you're <u>broken</u>, but this couldn't be further from the truth. Seeing a therapist is a sign that you care about yourself enough to get help when it's useful, and that's a good thing.

32. MAKE CHANGES ALONG THE WAY

Quit seeking validation all the time and embrace your crazy. This is your life. It's yours, because no one else has had the vision you did to start it. Stop seeking validation before you launch a new product, program or idea. The most successful people are those who were once believed to be crazy.

Celebrate even the smallest of wins. To maintain a go-getter attitude requires positive reinforcement. Have you worked up the courage to make that call you've been putting off. Did you finally get through that stack of seemingly, endless paperwork? Kick up your heels and celebrate. That energy will carry you forward.

Get specific on what you are attempting to accomplish. Now that you're trusting your own instincts and celebrating along the way, challenge yourself to break down your vision into smaller chunks. You need to stick to a plan. What do you want to achieve this month and what do you need to do this week to reach your goals?

As we know, writing your goals down significantly increases your chances of success. Know that making money is like making broccoli. A mentor once told me this. You're not afraid of using up the broccoli in your fridge, are you? You know you can always get more.

Similarly, if you're committed to growing into your new self, you can't be afraid to invest in your growth or do the things that excite you. Rather than worry about the money you're spending, focus on

164

making each investment worthwhile. Gentleness of spirit is the sure path to humility.

33. BECOME UNSTOPPABLE

If you feel like you really have done something great, chances are people will have already begun to notice that. Then they will come to respect you even more for your humility. This doesn't mean you should lie about achieving something. If someone asked if you ran a marathon, then it's perfectly acceptable to say yes.

Some people think that being a good person is as simple as not doing harm to another. But it is not always about what you don't do, but what you do for others. Being a good person also includes helping yourself as much as others. You have to decide what you believe being a good person entails. What personal traits is your ideal person consisting of?

Let it go. Seriously, relax, take a deep breath and just let go of holding on to life so tightly. You don't need to be all things to all people or please everyone at all times. Give yourself permission to decide that you're doing the best you can. Remind yourself when you're doing things well. Don't wait to hear it from someone else.

Make a list of traits that you believe make up a good, ideal person. Start living your life according to these traits. Are you waiting for something in return? Are you doing things because it will help you look good? Or are you doing things because you truly want to give and help. Stop putting up fake airs and adopt the attitude of giving without expectation of receiving anything in return.

Avoid bragging. It's okay to have a healthy self-esteem and to feel proud of your accomplishments, but nobody likes it when someone constantly tries to bring attention to themselves and their own achievements. Don't constantly talk about how absolutely amazing you were for running the marathon, or achieving other goals. This gets old fast and people will stop listening.

Don't take all the credit. We are human beings and who we are now has a lot to do with other people's influence and guidance. Countless people have given you support and helped you to become the person you are so that you can achieve your dreams.

It's totally fine to be proud about your achievements, but keep in mind that nobody ever does anything totally by themselves, and that as people, we are all helping each other to accomplish our goals. Share the love. Recognize others who have helped you on your path to success.

Take action without thinking, all too often, that you have a wonderful idea that's going to change the world (or at minimum, your world). Then the **voice of reason** comes in. Sometimes it's our own voice. Sometimes it's from peers or family. The problem with the **voice of reason** is that it's often lame, boring, lacks any sense of adventure and is WRONG.

Use <u>fear</u> to guide your actions. Sit back, and grab a piece of paper and a pencil. Answer the following question based on your gut instinct: What are you deathly afraid to do? I'm not talking about a little bit afraid. I'm talking about pee your pants level of scared. What is it? Fear is an indicator that something truly matters to you. Therefore, you must identify that which you fear and then do it.

CLOSING

Are you ready to create the new life you deserve? Taking action to apply all the ideas I shared in this book will help send you on the right path. You will find yourself breaking through barriers that you have been stuck at. Perhaps for the first time in years or maybe ever, you will find that you can start living the life of your dreams.

Let my words inspire you and remember that I am just a vessel spreading the truth directed to me from GOD. Creating the new life which you want so badly, this is not just a product of you doing it all by yourself. GOD is always there to assist you every step of the way. Never forget this as you lean on him for support and guidance through prayer and your faith.

It is now your time to shine. Start your new life full of encouragement. Use the power of a fresh perspective which you have gained via this book as well as other resources you are aligning yourself with. Never look back and never again put yourself in a position to feel so disempowered and helpless. You are powerful. Be Amazing and live the life you want starting right now. Move forward with joy and love in your heart.

Thank You!

Dayssy Davila

ABOUT THE AUTHOR

Dayssy Davila is an Ecuador born female entrepreneur and CEO/President for a non-profit organization, Family Law Community, which is helping and assisting victims of Domestic Violence.

Learn more about Dayssy at:

Amazon.com/author/dayssydavila (case sensitive)

Learn more about Dayssy's non-profit organization at:

FamilyCommunity.org

NOTE FROM THE PUBLISHER

i Master Life
EMPOWERING . ENGAGING . TRANSFORMING

Thank you for purchasing this **i Master Life Publishing** book. Our goal is to get high quality <u>Life Mastery</u> materials and other worthwhile media into the hands of incredible people like you.

FOLLOW US:

Join our mailing list and get updates on new releases, deals, bonus content and other great publications from **i Master Life Publishing**.

iMasterLife.com/fan

SUPPORT US:

If you enjoyed this or any of our other books, would you please help support **I Master Life**. The sustainable revenue you provide ensures we can continue to provide publishing the very best media possible for you.

Just go to this link:

iMasterLife.com/fund

Thank You!

Marc A. Shamus
Founder

MAY I ASK YOU FOR A FAVOR

If you enjoyed this book Starting a New Life Full of Encouragement or found it useful, I'd be very grateful if you'd post a short review on the Book site you purchased at.

Your support really does make a difference and I read all the reviews personally so I can get your feedback and make this book even better.

If you'd like to leave a review, then all you need to do is click on the appropriate link below and fill out a review.

iMasterLife.com/Reviews/Davila

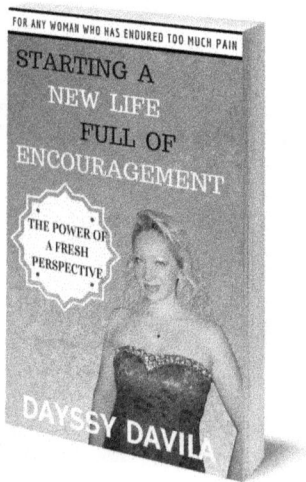

Thanks again for your support!

www.ingramcontent.com/pod-product-compliance
Lightning Source LLC
Chambersburg PA
CBHW071125280326
41935CB00010B/1116